CHRISTIAN HEROES: THEN & NOW

ALBERT SCHWEITZER

Le Grand Docteur

CHRISTIAN HEROES: THEN & NOW

ALBERT SCHWEITZER

Le Grand Docteur

JANET & GEOFF BENGE

YWAM Publishing is the publishing ministry of Youth With A Mission (YWAM), an international missionary organization of Christians from many denominations dedicated to presenting Jesus Christ to this generation. To this end, YWAM has focused its efforts in three main areas: (1) training and equipping believers for their part in fulfilling the Great Commission (Matthew 28:19), (2) personal evangelism, and (3) mercy ministry (medical and relief work).

For a free catalog of books and materials, call (425) 771-1153 or (800) 922-2143. Visit us online at www.ywampublishing.com.

Albert Schweitzer: Le Grand Docteur

Published by YWAM Publishing
a ministry of Youth With A Mission
P.O. Box 55787, Seattle, WA 98155-0787

Library of Congress Cataloging-in-Publication Data is on file.

ISBN 978-1-57658-961-8 (paperback)
ISBN 978-1-57658-004-6 (e-book)

First printing 2020

Printed in the United States of America

Christian Heroes: Then & Now

Adoniram Judson
Albert Schweitzer
Amy Carmichael
Betty Greene
Brother Andrew
Cameron Townsend
Charles Mulli
Clarence Jones
Corrie ten Boom
Count Zinzendorf
C. S. Lewis
C. T. Studd
David Bussau
David Livingstone
Dietrich Bonhoeffer
D. L. Moody
Elisabeth Elliot
Eric Liddell
Florence Young
Francis Asbury
George Müller
Gladys Aylward
Helen Roseveare
Hudson Taylor
Ida Scudder
Isobel Kuhn
Jacob DeShazer
Jim Elliot
John Flynn
John Newton
John Wesley
John Williams
Jonathan Goforth
Klaus-Dieter John
Lillian Trasher
Loren Cunningham
Lottie Moon
Mary Slessor
Mildred Cable
Nate Saint
Norman Grubb
Paul Brand
Rachel Saint
Richard Wurmbrand
Rowland Bingham
Samuel Zwemer
Sundar Singh
Wilfred Grenfell
William Booth
William Carey

Available in paperback, e-book, and audiobook formats.Unit study curriculum guides are available for select biographies.

www.YWAMpublishing.com

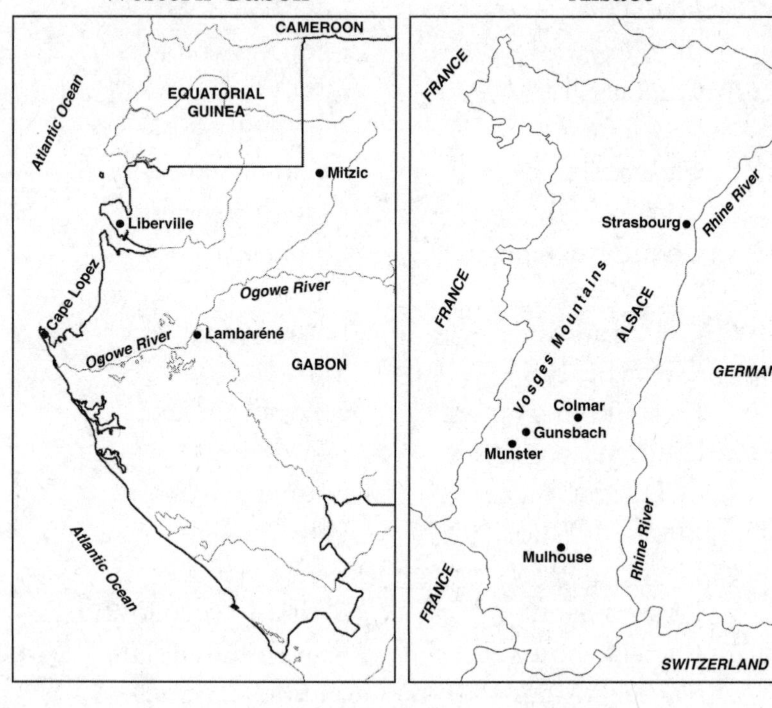

Western Gabon
CAMEROON
EQUATORIAL
GUINEA
Atlantic Ocean
Mitzic
Liberville
Cape Lopez
Ogowe River
Lambaréné
Ogowe River
GABON
Atlantic Ocean
Alsace
FRANCE
Strasbourg
Rhine River
FRANCE
Vosges Mountains
ALSACE
GERMANY
Colmar
Gunsbach
Munster
Mulhouse
Rhine River
FRANCE
SWITZERLAND

Contents

Chapter 1

Change of Circumstance

Icy rain fell as Albert Schweitzer trudged on. Following orders, he and his wife, Hélène, were walking from the Port of the Moon in the heart of Bordeaux, France, two miles south to a building on a narrow road. Albert's hands were burning from the string wrapped around the package of important books he was carrying. But he was more concerned about his wife. They both wore thin linen clothing suitable for Equatorial Africa, but the temperature in Bordeaux was 45 degrees Fahrenheit and Hélène shivered uncontrollably. As they walked, passersby jeered at them. At one point Hélène collapsed from exhaustion, or at least Albert hoped it was only exhaustion. He helped her up, wanting to believe they would be able to rest and recover and change into warm clothing when they got to their destination.

At last they arrived at the gate in front of a two-story white stone structure. A guard told them it was to be their temporary prison until they were transferred elsewhere. The wrought-iron gate slammed hard behind them as they walked up to the door of the building. After stepping inside, Albert's shoulders slumped. He and Hélène were taken to a drafty room with bare stone walls and floors and no heating. Accustomed to the heat and humidity of living just below the equator, Albert felt as though they'd been dumped into a freezer.

As days passed in the frigid conditions, Hélène's cough grew worse. Albert could hear the telltale symptoms of tuberculosis. Then they both fell ill with dysentery, something Albert had taken great pains to avoid during his four and a half years in Africa. Languishing in their cold room, Albert wondered where he and his wife would be transferred. Would they be separated? Sent deeper into France? Or worse, shipped to the rumored holding camp for enemy aliens in Egypt? He didn't know—he just hoped and prayed he and Hélène could stay together.

Sitting with his back against the wall and shivering, Albert reflected on his change of circumstance. He'd been a respected doctor sent out by a reputable French missionary society to work in Africa. Now he and his wife were detained enemy aliens in France. What madness had overtaken the world that led to his being held prisoner as an enemy of the country he loved? The one place Albert loved more than any other was Alsace, and he wondered if he would ever see his homeland again. Slowly his mind drifted to memories of life growing up there.

Chapter 2

Gunsbach

For probably the first time in his four years of life, Albert stood still while Gretel, the Schweitzer family's maid, brushed his wiry black hair. He didn't want to jeopardize the promise that he could attend church this morning like a big boy. So he didn't wiggle and complain as he usually did, even though having his hair brushed was one of the biggest trials of Albert's day. Gretel smeared oil on his hair and dragged the brush through it over and over again until she sighed and dredged up a part with a wooden pick. Her efforts hardly made a difference. Albert knew that within an hour his unruly hair would be as wild as before. The maid was right. Albert's hair was impossible to tame.

Albert looked at his older sister, Louisa, whose hair hung in two perfectly formed braids, just as it always did.

"Now for the bow tie," Albert heard Gretel say as she reached around to loop a silk tie behind his neck. "Remember, your papa says you're old enough for church now, but you must sit quietly and watch what the others do. If they stand, you stand. If they sit, you sit. No daydreaming."

Albert nodded. Almost every day Gretel and his mother told him to stop daydreaming, whether he was rocking his baby sister Emma's cradle or standing on a stool stirring a pot of lentils on the woodstove.

Adele Schweitzer, Albert's mother, walked into the room and spoke to Louisa. "Mind you sit up straight and listen to every word your papa says. And make sure Albert does the same. I expect a good report from Gretel on the both of you."

Five-year-old Louisa nodded.

Even though the Lutheran church that Albert's father pastored was just a few doors from the Schweitzer home, Albert felt the thrill of a new adventure. He was finally old enough to go to a church service. Of course, he'd been there many times when the congregation wasn't present. His father, the Reverend Louis Schweitzer, often let Albert sit at the back of the church and listen as Father Iltis practiced the weekly hymns on the pipe organ in the loft above. Albert loved those times when the organ echoed off the stone walls and sunlight shone through the church's stained-glass windows and danced on the floor.

Albert waved to his mother as he stepped outside. Adele was staying home to look after the baby. Emma was sickly, and Adele often stayed indoors to watch her. His two other sisters, two-year-old Marguerite and three-year-old Adele, clung to their mother's long blue skirt. Albert smiled. He was finally going somewhere with Louisa and leaving his three younger sisters behind. Louisa took Albert's hand, and together they walked down the cobblestone street and up the slope to the church.

A feeling of pride flooded Albert as he saw his father standing at the open door of the church, wearing his cassock and preaching bands. He smiled as he shook Albert's hands. "Be good in church and do what Gretel tells you to," he said.

Albert and Louisa settled into a pew near the front, on the women's side of the church. Gretel slid in beside them. As the congregation stood to sing a hymn, Albert looked around and listened closely to the sound of the pipe organ. He'd heard Father Iltis play the instrument many times before, but there was something special in hearing the notes carry loud and clear above the congregation's singing.

After the hymns had been sung, Albert's father climbed the stairs to the ornately carved pulpit that towered above the pews and began delivering the morning homily. He preached in German, though like most of their neighbors, the Schweitzers spoke Alsatian at home and sometimes French. It had been like that since before Albert was born, and it seemed perfectly natural for him to understand and speak all three languages.

Albert listened to the sermon for a few minutes and then turned his attention to the stained-glass windows. He'd overheard his father talking to his grandfather about how most Lutheran churches did not have such ornate windows. But the church in the village of Gunsbach, on the banks of the River Fecht, was different from others. It stood in the Alsace Valley between the beautiful Vosges Mountains to the west and the Rhine River to the east.

Once, when Albert found a piece of flint in the garden of their home, his father had explained that it was from Roman times, and that for over a thousand years the Alsace Valley had been a battleground for control of the region. The stained-glass windows represented part of that struggle. In 1639 the French gained control of the Alsace region. Several years later, King Louis XIV of France, who was Catholic, decreed that the German-style Lutherans could stay in their church buildings if they agreed to share them with Catholics. Along with this came a decree to install Catholic stained-glass windows in the churches and place a golden cross on the altar with statues of Mary and Joseph on either side. And that was how the front of the Gunsbach church remained laid out over two hundred years later.

Despite his young age, Albert had heard stories of how some Lutheran and Catholic clergy fought over church buildings. He remembered a funny story his father had told about how, long ago, a Lutheran pastor and a Catholic priest had both set the same time for their Sunday services. Since neither would back down, the priest and the pastor preached at the same time, trying to shout over each other.

No such thing happened in Gunsbach, however. Albert's father was a peace-loving man who gladly shared his church with Catholics, despite the fact that eight years earlier, Alsace had been annexed by the kingdom of Prussia after France had been defeated in the Franco-Prussian War, and the old French edict about sharing churches was no longer enforced. On the occasions when the Catholic priest was out of the village, Albert's father even visited sick parishioners for him.

Since he behaved so well during the service, Albert got to go to church every Sunday and also attend the missionary meetings his father held once a month. These meetings astonished Albert. He especially loved it when his father read stories from the Paris Evangelical Missionary Society's magazine. Many of them were about missionaries in Africa, and as his father read the stories aloud, Albert tried hard to imagine African people living among lions and elephants.

Not long afterward, Albert's mother took him to visit his great-aunt in Colmar, ten miles to the east. It was a Thursday—market day—and after Aunt Julie had purchased some vegetables, the family strolled down Kleberstrausse to the Champ de Mars memorial garden for war heroes. Albert looked up to see a tall bronze statue of Admiral Armand Joseph Bruat, commander of the French fleet during the Crimean War from 1853–1856. Around the bottom of the statue were four stone figures representing the four corners of the world. Albert walked around the base of the statue and studied each figure. He stopped for a long time in front of the statue of the African man with his head bent in surrender.

"Ah, you appreciate a great statue," Aunt Julie said. "This represents two famous men from Colmar: Admiral Bruat, and the sculptor, Frédéric Auguste Bartholdi. We can walk back past the house Bartholdi grew up in if you like."

Albert nodded, though it was hard for him to leave the statue of the African man. Something about the man's expression captivated Albert.

Another incident in Colmar also left a deep impression on Albert. On the way back to his great-aunt's house, he saw an injured horse. One man was dragging the animal by its bridle while another whipped its back and cursed. As soon as Albert asked his mother why they were mistreating the horse, he wished he hadn't. His mother explained that the horse was on its way to the slaughterhouse.

That night when Adele Schweitzer came in to say prayers with Albert, he added a silent prayer. "Dear God, please protect and bless all things that breathe, keep all evil from them, and let them sleep in peace." Even so, for weeks Albert couldn't stop thinking about the needless cruelty he had witnessed. He could not understand why anyone had to make an innocent animal suffer a beating.

Soon after Albert returned from the visit to Colmar, his father sat him down at the old upright piano in the living room. Albert knew it had belonged to his grandfather, Pastor Johann Schillinger, his mother's father. His parents had inherited the instrument before Albert was born, when his grandfather died. The piano didn't make the same impressive, swelling sound as the church organ, but most evenings after dinner Louis Schweitzer played hymns and songs on it for the children. From the time Albert could stand up and reach the keys, he'd enjoyed pretending to play the piano. By now he could pick out simple tunes with his right hand. His father told him he'd decided it was time to show Albert how to use his left hand to make chords on the keyboard. Louis sat down beside his son and patiently explained how he would have to learn which groups of notes sounded good together. Part of that meant playing scales. Once he could play scales, he could use them to pick out the chords with his left hand while playing the melody with his right. It wasn't difficult. Albert hadn't expected it to be. After all, he came from a long line of organ players on both sides of his family. Within a few weeks, Albert could play many hymns with both hands. He also dreamed of playing the church organ one day.

In the fall of 1880, Albert began attending school, something he'd dreaded. He couldn't think of anything worse than being crammed into one room five days a week, staring at a slate and trying to produce letters and numbers on it with a piece of chalk. Louisa brought her slate home every night, and Albert's mother often complimented her on how round and regular her letters were. Albert had a gloomy feeling he wouldn't be anywhere near as good as his sister.

On the first day of school, Albert cried all the way there. His teacher, Fraulein Goguel, directed him to sit next to another boy. Albert recognized him as the butcher's son, but didn't know his name. Although Gunsbach was a small village, Albert's mother had always forbade her children to play with other village children. When Albert questioned her about this, she explained that being a pastor's son was an important position in the village and he could not make friends with the farmer's son or the blacksmith's son. Now that Albert was in school with these boys and girls, he had no idea how to make friends with any of them.

After the school bell rang, the children sat at their desks and recited the alphabet. Within minutes Albert's mind began drifting. He wasn't in the classroom anymore. Instead he was sitting on his favorite rock, looking out at the ruins of Schwartzenbourg Castle farther up the valley.

"Albert, didn't you hear me say it was your turn to come to the front?" Fraulein Goguel said, her stern words breaking into his daydreaming. Albert scrambled to his feet as the boy seated behind him snickered.

During breaks, Albert stood alone. He only had sisters, and most of them were younger. He didn't know how to play with other boys. Instead he looked up to the Vosges Mountains, wishing he were there and not standing in the schoolyard.

On his first afternoon at school, they had singing class. The music teacher played one note at a time on the harmonium as she encouraged the children to sing German folk songs. Albert was puzzled. The single notes were jarring. He thought it would be much better if the teacher played with both hands, as his father had taught him to do.

When singing class was over, Albert couldn't contain himself. "Why do you play with only one finger at a time?" he asked the teacher. She looked surprised, and Albert felt he had to explain further. "Like this," he said, sliding onto the stool at the harmonium. Thinking back to the last folk song they had sung, he played the melody with his right hand and the accompanying chords with his left. It sounded much more beautiful to him than the single notes the teacher had played. When Albert finished, he turned to the teacher to see if he had gotten the point across. The music teacher had a strange look on her face, as if Albert had done something odd. He felt his face turn red.

As the weeks went by, the music teacher's harmonium playing did not improve, and it dawned on Albert that that might be the best she could do. Five-year-old Albert felt embarrassed when he realized that, without trying, he had surpassed his music teacher at the keyboard. He hadn't meant to humiliate an adult, and he determined not to shine in class again.

Not long after, however, Fraulein Goguel told the class the story of Noah's Ark and the flood. This was a subject Albert considered himself somewhat of an expert on. His father had told him the story several times, and since the summer before had been particularly wet, Albert had witnessed what happens when it rains for what seems like all day and all night for forty days. The village didn't fill up with water, but the rain ran down the cobblestone streets and into the river. How then, Albert asked his father, was the rain that fell for forty days and forty nights enough to flood the entire world? His father smiled. "At that time, at the beginning of the world, the rain did not come down in drops the way it does now. It came down in bucketfuls."

Since the answer made perfect sense to Albert, when he heard his teacher tell the story and omit the part about bucketfuls of rain, he couldn't help but interrupt her. "Teacher, you must tell the story correctly. You must say that at that time the rain came down in bucketfuls, not drops. That way there was enough rain in forty days to cover the whole earth."

The teacher looked oddly at Albert. Once again Albert had the feeling he did not fit into his class. None of the other boys or girls seemed at all concerned about how much water fell from the sky. *Why,* he asked himself, *did it bother him*?

Chapter 3

Fitting In

Over the next several weeks, Albert tried to make friends at school. Sometimes the other boys let him play with them, but he always felt they only tolerated him. This led him to try harder to fit in, even when he didn't feel good about it afterward.

One afternoon, Albert was walking home from school with several other boys. One of them starting yelling, "Mausche, Mausche, go away!" Albert looked behind him to see a bent old man leading a donkey cart along the main thoroughfare through Gunsbach. Another of the boys joined the chant, and then another. They folded the corners of their jackets to look like pigs' ears and began walking alongside the old man leading the cart. At first Albert was shocked that schoolboys would act in such a disrespectful way toward an old man, but somehow an irresistible pull to be like the other boys overcame him. Soon Albert was also yelling, "Mausche, Mausche, go away!" and watching gleefully as several of the boys picked up stones and pelted the old Jewish man as he passed on down the road.

That night in bed, Albert thought about what he'd done. He tried to remember everything his father preached about Jews. They were God's chosen people. Moses was a Jew, as were King David and many other heroes of the Old Testament. As far as Albert could remember, Mausche was the first Jewish person he had seen, and he looked like so many other old men in the village. So why did the boys hate him? And why did Albert himself join them in yelling at the defenseless old man? Albert had even felt a tinge of joy in joining in with the others. For once he was one of the boys, united against a common enemy. But that realization made him feel even more ashamed of his actions, and he promised himself never again to yell at the old man if he came back through the village.

School was hard, but home was difficult too. When Albert was seven, his youngest sister Emma died. Her death haunted him. She had been a sickly baby, but so had he. Albert's mother often told the story of how, when he was six months old, they had moved from Kayserberg to Gunsbach. One day after their arrival, the church women came to meet their new pastor and his family. Albert was puny and yellow. Albert's mother said she overheard a woman say that the first service Pastor Schweitzer would likely hold in Gunsbach would be the funeral for his baby son. When Albert's mother heard the comment, she fled the room in tears and refused to return to the "welcome" gathering. And now, as they prepared for Emma's funeral service, Albert wondered why his life had been spared and hers taken. Why did God allow some people to die and others to live? Albert wanted to ask his father about it, but he was too shy to do so.

Albert also wondered about Uncle Albert Schillinger, after whom he was named. Uncle Albert was his mother's brother and had been the pastor at the Church of St. Nicholas in Strasbourg. In 1870, five years before Albert's birth, the Germans were preparing to invade Strasbourg. Uncle Albert offered to journey to Paris to gather medical supplies in preparation for the battle. He managed to collect the supplies, but as he tried to return, he learned that the Germans had already surrounded Strasbourg, and his beloved city was under siege. The Germans captured and imprisoned Uncle Albert, but the supplies he had procured in Paris were allowed into the city.

When the war was over, Uncle Albert returned to pastor his church, but soon afterward he collapsed and died. Albert's mother often told her brother's story, adding that she hoped Albert would be worthy of his name and grow up to be a scholar and hero like his uncle. But Albert wondered about it all. Why would God allow Uncle Albert to survive the war, only to to drop dead when it was over? It seemed impossible to think of a good reason why that had happened.

One month after Emma's burial, Albert's mother gave birth to another baby. This time it was a boy, whom his parents named Paul. Albert was surprised. He was so used to sisters that it was hard to imagine having a brother. But there he was, healthy and strong, lying in Emma's old crib.

Despite his unhappiness at school, Albert still had to attend classes. As he glumly counted up, Albert realized he might have twelve more years of education stretching out in front of him. He could hardly imagine that. It seemed like an eternity. Very slowly and with a lot of repetition, Albert learned to read and write and to do simple addition and subtraction. His letters and numbers were clumsy, and his teachers always told him he could do better if he just concentrated more. Albert tried, yet he couldn't help but feel he did not fit in at school, at home, or anywhere. He was bigger and stronger than other boys his age, but what use was that when he was sitting behind a desk?

On Albert's way home from school one day an older boy, George Nitschelm, challenged him to a wrestling match. Albert agreed. Both boys put down their slates, stripped off their shirts, and wrestled by the side of the road. Even though George was older and taller, Albert was a natural wrestler, and he won the contest. As Albert pinned George down, George looked up at him and hissed, "Of course you won. If I had meat twice a week like you, I'd be as strong as you are." Albert was mortified. He thought he was making progress at being accepted by the other boys, but apparently not.

That night when his mother placed a pot of steaming chicken soup on the table, Albert pushed his bowl away. It reminded him of every way he was different from the other boys. He knew he would have to take decisive action if he didn't want to be an outsider all his life.

One thing separating Albert from the rest of the boys at school was the clothes he wore. His mother took great care to make sure he was always well-dressed. Unlike the other boys, Albert often wore a starched-collar shirt to school along with leather boots. But Albert knew that would have to stop. The following morning, he dressed in his oldest pair of trousers, pulled on a plain brown smock, threw his boots under the bed, and pulled out a pair of wooden clogs like the other boys wore. He had to admit they weren't as comfortable as the leather boots his grandfather had given him, but Albert didn't mind. All he wanted was to fit in.

"What do you think you are wearing?" Albert's mother said in a raised voice when he came downstairs for breakfast. "Your father has already left for Colmar, but he would tell you the same thing. Go right back upstairs and change into your school clothes. Do you want to disgrace our family?"

Albert certainly didn't want to do that, but more than anything, he wanted friends at school. So he stood his ground. "This is what the other boys wear, Mama."

"You're not the other boys. Go upstairs and change," she retorted.

Albert ignored her and sat down at the table, knowing he wouldn't win a verbal argument with his mother, yet doubting she would actually carry him upstairs and change his clothes.

That day Albert wore his "peasant outfit" to school, and he was pleased that he looked more like the other boys. But it came at a price. That night, after Albert's father returned from Colmar, he took Albert down to the basement and demanded an explanation about the clothes he had worn to school. Although Albert shook with fear, he refused to back down. His father slapped him across the side of the face and locked him in the basement to think about the sin of disobeying his parents, but Albert didn't care. At school, he wasn't going to look like the privileged son of a pastor ever again. The situation went on for several weeks. Albert would come downstairs wearing his oldest clothes, and his mother would nag him while his father slapped him and banished him to the basement. Eventually, they reached a compromise. Albert could wear his old clothes to school but on Sundays or when they had guests at the house, he'd wear his best clothes.

Every time Albert got a new item of clothing, the disagreement was revived. At the start of winter his father got a new overcoat, and a tailor cut up the old one and reworked it into a smaller overcoat for Albert. But none of the other schoolboys wore overcoats, so Albert refused to wear it. His mother knitted him warm woolen gloves, but the boys wore fingerless ones. His aunt wanted to buy him a sailor hat, but his classmates all wore brown woolen caps. On and on it went. Even though he was only seven years old, Albert was a stubborn match for his parents.

Throughout the struggle, Albert felt himself getting closer to being accepted by the other boys at school. That is, until Heinrich Brasch invited him to make slingshots together and go bird hunting. It was spring, and Albert was glad to be included in Heinrich's plans. They made their way through the terraced vineyards surrounding Gunsbach and onto the gentle slope above the village. There they hunted for forked sticks suitable for slingshots.

When Albert found the perfect stick, he pulled out an India-rubber band his mother had given him. As he wound it around the ends of the fork, he thought about the slingshot he was making. It had started as a stick—part of a tree a bird might perch on—but now he was fashioning it into a weapon to kill birds with. Albert hated the thought. What had any bird ever done to him that it deserved being killed for? Why should he or anyone else take away a bird's life—its right to sing and eat and fly free? He imagined telling Heinrich that he didn't want to make the weapon and didn't want to kill anything, but he was too afraid to say so. What would happen at school if he did? Would the older boys tease him for being a coward who wouldn't even kill a bird?

As he finished winding the rubber band around the forked stick, Albert prayed that God would warn any birds in the area to flee for their lives. It didn't work. "Look," Heinrich whispered, nudging Albert's elbow. "There's a flock of stonechats on the beech tree over there. Let's creep a bit closer and get them." Albert looked up with dread and saw about thirty stonechats resting on the limbs of the newly budding tree.

Albert watched Heinrich pull two small pebbles from his pocket. "Come on," he whispered. "Let's shoot them at the same time." Albert reached for the pebbles he'd collected and set one in the cradle of his slingshot. Just then, the bells of his father's church rang out, reminding the congregation that it was Lent. To Albert it felt like a jolt went through his body. He heard the bells chime but also heard the words of the sixth commandment, "Thou shalt not kill," run through his mind. Albert dropped his slingshot as though it were a hot coal and ran toward the stonechats in the beech tree, waving both his hands. "Go! Go! Go!" he yelled. The birds rose together into the air and flew off.

His face red with anger, Heinrich turned to Albert. "What did you do that for, you idiot? I had a good shot lined up."

Albert didn't answer. Instead he left his slingshot on the ground and ran home. That night in bed, as he said his prayer for the protection of all animals, Albert knew he'd made an important decision that afternoon. He had chosen to stand up for what he believed was right, even if it meant losing the friendships he had so painfully cultivated with his classmates.

After the bird-hunting incident, Albert spent even more time alone. When he had finished his after-school chores, his mother would let him play outside. Albert's favorite pastime soon became wandering the hills above the village, studying rocks and birds' nests, and, of course, daydreaming.

Occasionally something would happen in Gunsbach that drew the entire town together. One of those things happened on a school day. Albert was on the playground when he heard an uproar. He and the other children ran to the wall and peered over. Leaning against the wall of the inn next door was a strange contraption with one large wheel at the front and one much smaller wheel at the rear. "It's a high-wheel bicycle," one of the boys said. "My father saw someone riding one in Strasbourg last month."

While Albert had heard of a high-wheel bicycle, he'd never seen one before. Now, staring over the wall at one, he wondered if such an ungainly contraption would really take the place of horses, as his mother predicted.

A crowd gathered around the inn entrance, waiting for the rider to finish his wine. The schoolchildren joined them. When the owner of the high-wheel bicycle emerged from the inn, the whole crowd, including seven-year-old Albert, laughed out loud. The man was wearing short pants and was undeterred by the laughter. He wheeled the bicycle into the street, held the handlebars atop the large front wheel, put one foot on the metal spike at the back, and scooted forward with the other foot. When he'd gathered enough speed, he quickly slid up into the seat, put his feet onto the pedals that connected directly to the large front wheel, and pedaled down the street. Albert was impressed by the man's agility, but he wasn't sure that high-wheel bicycles were the future of transportation.

That Christmas, 1882, Albert learned that a price had to be paid for receiving presents. Several of his aunts and uncles, along with his godparents, had sent him Christmas gifts. Until now he'd loved opening them, especially the books with pictures of nature or faraway places in them. But now his father declared that Albert was old enough to write his own thank-you notes. His father required the notes to include three parts. First, Albert had to directly thank the person who gave the gift, assuring him or her that it was just what he'd wanted and that it brought him much pleasure. Then he was to outline for the person all the other gifts he had received. Finally, he was to wish the person a happy New Year. He also had to write a draft of each thank-you note on a sheet of paper for his father to look over and correct. Then he was to rewrite the note on a clean sheet of paper with no spelling or grammar errors and no accidental ink blots on the page. The whole ordeal was a challenge for Albert, who began to wonder if he might end up locked in his father's study until the following Christmas to finish the task.

It was hard work, but Albert managed to get the thank-you notes written before his eighth birthday rolled around on January 14. For his birthday Albert had requested a New Testament of his own from his father. Although writing neatly was a terrible burden, as demonstrated by the thank-you notes, by now Albert could read well and wanted to read the Bible for himself.

Albert set himself the task of reading the entire New Testament. As he read, he had many questions for his father—questions he was surprised no one else was asking. How was it, for instance, that Jesus's family was poor when the wise men had brought Him gold, frankincense, and myrrh? Wasn't that enough to make them rich? What did they do with those things? And what did the shepherds in the fields do after seeing the angels the night Jesus was born? Did they try to track Jesus down to see why God had sent an angel to tell of His birth? Albert had a thousand such questions and was thankful that his father, who had a theology degree from Strasbourg University, was happy to try to answer them for him.

Another wonderful event occurred when Albert was eight years old—something that gave him a greater opportunity to concentrate on music. By now he could play complicated tunes on the piano, and his father promised he would ask Father Iltis to teach Albert to play the church pipe organ one day. During summer of 1883, that day came. Albert climbed the stairs at the back of the church to the loft that housed the controls and the keyboards, or manuals as they were known, for the organ. He slid onto the bench next to Father Iltis in front of the manuals. His feet barely touched the organ's pedals as he studied the two rows of white and black keys and the rows of stops on either side of the manuals. Father Iltis explained how the stops were used to make particular sounds and how the two manuals and the pedals worked together. Then he played a tune. Albert listened as the sound reverberated from the organ pipes above him. He was so close to the instrument that he could feel the sound vibrate through him, as though the music had taken control of his body. Soon Father Iltis had Albert playing simple tunes on the organ. As he played, Albert felt a strange oneness with the organ, as if the instrument had been made just for him.

Chapter 4

Trapped

During autumn 1884, life changed for nine-year-old Albert. He knew it would. It was time to leave the village school and continue his education at the realschule (secondary school) in Munster, two and a half miles to the west. For Albert, the best thing about attending this new school was the fact that there were two walking paths from Gunsbach to Munster: the high path and the low path. The other village boys took the low path, since it was easier. Albert took the high path, leaving him with lots of time to daydream as he walked alone to school in the morning and back home in the late afternoon.

The walk became the highlight of Albert's day. Sometimes as he proceeded along the path he pretended to be a natural scientist, stopping to examine the blossoms on the cherry trees as they turned day by day into tiny fruits and then into delicious ripe cherries. He also tried composing poems and drawing sketches of the surrounding countryside. Both endeavors fell flat, and Albert decided he was neither a poet nor an artist. Sometimes he wondered what he would be when he grew up. Perhaps, he told himself, he would be a goatherd. What could be better than spending his days wandering among the hills and valleys throughout the seasons?

Realschule itself was a trial for Albert. He had to study Latin, which he hated, and complicated mathematics, which he disliked just as much. He also developed a new habit in class. Whenever the teacher called on him and he didn't know the answer to a question, he would laugh nervously, which annoyed the teacher yet amused the other boys. This left Albert with a reputation for not taking his schoolwork seriously.

After one year at the realschule, Albert knew he was in trouble with his parents. His report card noted that he laughed a lot in class and spent too much time looking out the window daydreaming. His teacher declared something had to change.

"I expected a lot better from you," Albert's father told him as they sat in his study. "Look at this report card. You're hardly passing your classes. At your age I was at a gymnasium, which was far more rigorous than realschule. You have the brains to do that too, just not the willpower. Why don't you understand how important it is to do well at school? If you don't learn to concentrate, you'll never make anything of your life."

Albert had nothing to say. He knew his father was right. Alsace had two types of secondary school: the realschule and the gymnasium. Realschule, such as the one in Munster, was for average students who might take up a trade when their studies ended. The gymnasium was a more rigorous school designed to prepare top students to sit the Abitur exam, which allowed them to go on to university. Yet Albert couldn't imagine going to university after nine long years of secondary school. He didn't really care what kind of education he got, though he could see that his attitude upset his parents, who certainly wanted him to do better.

"I have given this some thought," Albert's father continued. "It's time you grew up and learned to discipline yourself. Your Uncle Louis has stepped in and offered a way for you to redeem yourself. Next semester you are going to live with him and Aunt Sophie in Mulhouse, where you'll be attending a gymnasium." Albert's father paused and took a deep breath. "I expect you to rise to the occasion. Not every boy in Alsace gets such an opportunity, and certainly not one who doesn't concentrate on his schoolwork. But I think you can do it, as long as you apply yourself."

"Yes, sir," Albert replied mechanically, aware that in the past ten minutes his future had changed drastically.

That night in bed, Albert cried himself to sleep. How was he ever going to leave his sisters and brother and the mountains and valleys of Gunsbach to go and live thirty-five miles away in Mulhouse? Uncle Louis, the half brother of Grandfather Schweitzer, and Aunt Sophie had no children. Albert thought they were strict, humorless people and wondered how he would survive with them.

The next day, Albert begged his father to reconsider sending him to live with his uncle and aunt, but there was no way out. The gymnasium in Mulhouse offered several scholarships to the sons of pastors, and Uncle Louis, who was a school inspector, had secured one for Albert. That in itself was a gift, Albert's father pointed out, since his son's grades did not indicate he had the potential to go on to university. Albert stood glumly. It was over. For better or worse he was destined to spend the next nine years in Mulhouse.

Albert and his father rode the train south to Mulhouse in mid-October. As they rolled through the mountains and valleys and out onto the Rhine River plain, Albert hardly had the energy to look out the window. He was leaving behind everything he loved—wandering in the hills, sitting on his special rock, watching the storks return to nest in the church belfry. These and so many other enjoyable things would be replaced with more Latin, more mathematics, more sitting up straight at the table doing homework. The prospect was grim.

As district school inspector, Uncle Louis along with Aunt Sophie lived in an apartment attached to the high school. This meant that Albert would never be far from school—or his teachers, some of whom lived in surrounding apartments. As he lay in bed on his first night in Mulhouse, Albert went over the daily schedule that Aunt Sophie had laid out for him. He was to rise at 6:00 a.m. to wash and dress. Then it was breakfast, followed by chores around the house. Although school started at 8:00 a.m., Albert needed to be out of the apartment by 7:30 a.m. in order to be suitably early to class. He was to return to the apartment for lunch at 11:00 a.m. and use the rest of the lunch hour to practice piano. Then it was back to school at noon for two more hours of lessons. After school, according to his aunt, he was to come straight home and not dillydally in the street with other boys. Once home, Albert was to change his clothes, do more household chores, and be ready for coffee at 4:00 p.m. when Uncle Louis arrived home from work. After coffee Albert was to practice piano for another hour, followed by an hour of homework, which he was to do seated at the kitchen table with Aunt Sophie closely supervising.

The only time Albert had any choice about activities was between homework and dinner. Aunt Sophie told him that during that time he could read a book or one of the three newspapers delivered to the apartment. After dinner came more homework from 8:30 to 10:30, when everyone went to bed and the candles were blown out.

A tear slid down Albert's cheek. He had no idea how he would keep up with the new schedule. It was so different from his schedule back in Gunsbach. His mother had tried to get him to study, but the three younger children were always distracting her, leaving Albert at peace to daydream. In Mulhouse Albert felt trapped, as though he'd been sentenced to prison for the next nine years. He dreaded waking each morning to begin his grueling routine.

Just as Albert had predicted, his first week at school in Mulhouse went badly. He was behind in Latin and hadn't yet started Greek, as the other boys had. As a result, he had a lot of extra homework to catch up on. To make matters worse, Aunt Sophie was concerned that Albert play only with the "right" boys. According to her, only two boys in Albert's class were worthy of mixing with: Eduard Ostier and Pierre Matthieu. Pierre, a pastor's son, was also attending the gymnasium on a scholarship. Aunt Sophie told Albert that if any other boys invited him to play or study at their homes, he was to politely refuse. And he had no chance to meet other boys outside of school. His aunt didn't believe in free time to go running around outside. Such activity, she said, could lead a boy into mischief. All Albert could do was look longingly from the apartment to the mountains in the distance, knowing his family was experiencing a different life just a few hills and valleys to the north. It was all he could do to stop himself from running away.

On Sunday, Albert accompanied his uncle and aunt to St. Stephen's Church, a large, ornate building with a tall spire and five clanging bells in the bell tower. Albert immediately noticed the organ. It was bigger than the pipe organ in Gunsbach. This organ had three manuals and sixty-two stops. And although the organist had his back to the congregation, Albert could tell he played with vigor and flair. When Pastor Wennagel climbed the carved spiral stairs to the pulpit, Albert's mind drifted to the organist. He wondered how long the man had studied music before winning the coveted position as the organist of a beautiful church like this one.

The morning service at St. Stephen's was longer than Albert was used to. When it was over, Uncle Louis and Aunt Sophie gathered in the square outside and introduced Albert to their friends and acquaintances.

It was customary following lunch each Sunday for families to take a walk, during which Albert was confronted by the grimness of Mulhouse. The town was a leading center in textile production. The sooty brick walls of cotton mills, weaving sheds, and rows of brick chimneys spewing dark gray smoke dominated the town. Albert took several longing glances over his shoulder at the familiar mountains behind him.

After the walk Albert wondered whether he would ever be happy again. He felt sad being away from his family and felt sorry for himself because his schoolwork was piling up. Even music no longer brought him joy. Aunt Sophie, an accomplished pianist herself, supervised Albert's music lessons. At home he'd been free to improvise on his grandfather's old piano. No one minded if he added his own musical notes or changed the tempo. But Aunt Sophie was like a hawk. She sat beside Albert as he played, turning the sheet music and watching for any deviation from it. She insisted Albert spend most of his lessons sight-reading the music instead of playing by ear. Albert learned to hate the sight of his aunt's piano.

Winter term went by slowly, with each day seeming like the one before. Albert barely noticed the first snow as it fell over the town. It made him sad to think of how he and Louisa used to toboggan down the hill behind their father's church, or how his mother had hot soup waiting when he returned home from visiting the Fecht River to see how far it had iced over.

When December arrived, Albert expected that later in the month he would take the train back home on his own. He was surprised when instead his father showed up at Uncle Louis's apartment. His surprise turned to dread when he learned that the principal of the gymnasium had summoned his father for a meeting. Albert could only imagine what that would be about. His grades were at the bottom of his class, and he struggled with Greek and mathematics, two subjects he needed to pass to graduate. When the meeting was over, his father returned to the apartment holding Albert's report card. "We will not discuss this now," he said. "When we get home, I shall talk with your mother and decide what to do with you."

This sounded serious and cast a shadow over Albert's return home to his family for Christmas. Even the Christmas trappings—the tree in the living room decorated with candles and paper fans, the presents from various aunts and uncles spilling out underneath the tree, and the smell of the delicious meat pie his mother always prepared for special meals—couldn't dispel the cloud of gloom over Albert as he sensed that something bad was about to happen.

The day after Christmas, the older children—Louisa, Albert, and Adele—were called into their father's study and told to write thank-you letters for the presents they had received. As always, Albert found this a challenging chore. He marveled at the way Louisa could think of something different and interesting to write in each letter.

But worse news was to come. That night Albert's father called him back into his study. "I think you know why I was asked to speak to the principal," he began. Albert hung his head. "It appears you've made no effort to improve your schoolwork, so much so that the principal suggests we withdraw you from the gymnasium and allow your scholarship to be used by some boy who wants to improve himself."

Albert stared down at the rug on the study floor. Part of him was hopeful. Perhaps his time at the gymnasium was over. He could rejoin his sisters and brother and return to live in Gunsbach and make the walk to the realschule and back each day. How wonderful it would be to be back in nature.

"Many people are making sacrifices for you to go to the best school possible, and this is how you thank them," Albert's father continued, waving the report card at his son.

Albert swallowed hard. He thought of all the times Uncle Louis had patiently explained his mathematics homework to him or how Aunt Sophie had tested him on Latin declensions. Albert knew how much raising a son who was a scholar meant to his father. His Schweitzer ancestors had been teachers, pastors, and organists for as long as they had been keeping records. Albert, as the oldest son, had big shoes to fill. As much as he didn't want to fill them, Albert agreed to return to Mulhouse after Christmas and concentrate harder on his studies.

Chapter 5

Improvement

Following Christmas, Albert dutifully returned to his Aunt Sophie and Uncle Louis's apartment in Mulhouse. As the train rolled along, he tried to talk himself into working harder at school, but he didn't know how to do it. School subjects didn't interest Albert, and even piano lessons were drudgery under Aunt Sophie's stern direction. As he observed the countryside through the train window, Albert wished he could be free to wander in nature, free to sit on his favorite rock and think about things that interested him, free to compose the kind of music he liked to play on the piano. But none of that was possible. Albert stepped off the train at Mulhouse with a sense of dread.

On January 14, 1886, Albert turned eleven. A week later he returned to classes. Before Albert set out for school, Uncle Louis gave him a lecture on how it was time to grow up and take his responsibilities seriously. Back in class, as Albert tried hard to stay focused, he began noticing small changes. He started seeing connections between French and Latin. And when he studied botany, he remembered the shapes of flowers in the woods and how the flowers grew. Music remained a chore, yet Albert dared to dream that one day he would become an organist.

Each time Albert returned to Gunsbach during school vacations, he noticed his family seemed a little poorer than during his previous visit. His father's health was failing, and there was less wood to burn in the fireplace to keep the drafty old manse warm. His mother now seldom used butter in her cooking and darned socks that had already been mended. As he observed his family's deteriorating financial situation, Albert was grateful that his aunt and uncle provided him free room and board in Mulhouse. This spurred him to work harder at school, and his grades slowly improved.

Many books filled the bookshelves in Uncle Louis and Aunt Sophie's apartment. To his own astonishment, soon after his thirteenth birthday in 1888, Albert began reading through each book, one after the other. He also loved to read the three newspapers delivered each morning.

As 1888 progressed, Albert noticed some interesting headlines and stories in the newspapers. He watched as the "Year of the Three Kaisers" played out in the papers. On March 9, 1888, Wilhelm I died after a twenty-seven-year reign as king of Prussia and emperor of Germany. He was succeeded by his fifty-six-year-old son, Frederick III, whose wife Victoria was the eldest child of Great Britain's Queen Victoria. Frederick suffered from throat cancer, which left him unable to talk and forced him to write down all his instructions. Then in June 1888, after ruling ninety-nine days, Fredrick III died, and his twenty-nine-year-old son, Wilhelm II, ascended to the role of emperor or kaiser.

Albert found himself engrossed in other current events, wondering how they might change his life. He read in one newspaper about the first-ever road trip in a motor wagon. Bertha Benz, wife of Karl Benz, drove sixty-six miles from Mannheim to Pforzheim in twelve hours. Albert was amazed. He had been hoping to save enough money to buy a bicycle. Now he wondered if he would one day have to share the road with gasoline-powered horseless carriages.

Reading the newspaper became one of Albert's favorite pastimes. One day in autumn as he read the *Strasbourg Post,* he became aware that his aunt was watching him closely. One story Albert read in the *Post* was about a man dubbed Jack the Ripper. The article described how he murdered lone women on the streets of London, England, terrorizing the city in the process. At dinner, Aunt Sophie brought up the topic of what Albert was reading in the newspapers by saying, "Albert, I really don't think I can have you reading the newspapers anymore. You only read the sensational stories. I think you could make better use of your time reading classic novels."

Albert stared at his soup while he collected his thoughts. Was his aunt serious? Just two years before she'd been constantly nagging him because he didn't like to read anything. Now that he was reading the newspapers daily, she continued to complain. "Aunt Sophie," Albert began, "I've learned so many interesting things from the newspapers. It's like reading history, only when it's happening instead of twenty years afterward."

Aunt Sophie huffed. "I doubt you're reading current events," she replied. "I've watched the way you follow that awful story about the man murdering women in England."

Albert turned to his uncle. "Uncle Louis, surely you can see it's good for a young man to know what's going on in the world?"

Uncle Louis looked uncomfortable. Albert knew he rarely contradicted his wife. "Well . . . " he began after thinking a minute. "Let's put the boy to the test and see whether or not he's just reading the sensational parts of the newspapers. Albert, who are the princes of Greece?"

"Constantine, George, Nicholas, and Andrew," Albert replied.

"Quite right," Uncle Louis said with a nod. He went on to quiz Albert about the current ruler of the Balkans, the members of the French cabinet, and several other questions before he turned back to his wife. "Well, Sophie, I think the boy reads more than the gossip pages. He seems to have a firm grasp on what's happening in the world. I think he's making good use of the newspapers."

Aunt Sophie nodded, and Albert smiled to himself. He had impressed his uncle with his knowledge—something not easily done. From then on Albert was completely free to read the newspapers as he chose, and often during dinner he had long, interesting conversations with Uncle Louis about current events.

Aunt Sophie was still determined, however, to "improve" Albert's reading. The next thing she picked on was the way he read books. Aunt Sophie read a book slowly and methodically from cover to cover. Albert, on the other hand, read through a book haphazardly, skipping parts that didn't interest him and jumping from one part to another. If he liked what he read, he would go back and read the entire book. If he didn't like what he read, he quickly moved on to another book.

By now, judging from his aunt's frowning glances, Albert was aware that she didn't approve of his reading style. One evening as the two sat reading at the table, Aunt Sophie tackled the issue. "Albert, you must slow down when you read," she began. "You don't give yourself time to appreciate a book's style. That's the most important thing to consider and enjoy as you read. What you do is 'sniff' through a book as fast as you can, completely missing its style."

Albert took a deep breath, ready to reply, and then he thought better of it. Aunt Sophie considered herself an expert on the proper way to read a book, and he knew it was pointless to challenge her on it. "Yes, Aunt. Thank you for the advice," was all he said. But inside Albert knew exactly how to judge a book and its style. If, as he sniffed through it, he skipped over many sentences, paragraphs, or even whole pages, obviously the book's style was bad, and he didn't want to continue reading it. If he found himself not wanting to skip sentences and paragraphs, the book exhibited good style. It was simple to Albert, and he wondered why his aunt worried so much.

After church one Sunday morning, as they walked back to the apartment, Aunt Sophie brought up the topic of the new church organist. "He's very good, isn't he?"

"Yes," Albert replied. "I very much enjoyed listening to him play."

"His name is Herr Eugène Munch," Aunt Sophie continued. "He's come to St. Stephen's after studying music in Berlin. He is now accepting piano students. You will start lessons with him next Wednesday after school."

Albert was shocked. He could tell that Eugène Munch was a gifted organist. Perhaps one day, he told himself, Herr Munch would let him try playing St. Stephen's beautiful organ.

While Albert was glad to be free of Aunt Sophie's rigid music lessons, things didn't start out particularly well with Herr Munch. Albert's new teacher would assign him a piece of music to practice and play at their next class. But when Albert sat down at the piano at his uncle and aunt's apartment to practice, his mind wandered. He would find himself improvising and playing the music the way he wanted it to sound instead of how his teacher wanted it played.

One week, Albert was given a Mozart sonata to learn for his next lesson. As usual, his mind drifted off as he tried to learn the music. At the next music class as he played the sonata, Albert could tell by the way Herr Munch paced the floor and scowled that he wasn't happy with his playing. Finally, the music teacher let out a roar. "You have ruined my beautiful Mozart. Such wonderful music, and you play it like you are playing a barrel organ." With that, Herr Munch snatched the music from the piano so quickly that it looked like the pince-nez eye glasses perched precariously on the bridge of his nose might fly off.

"What can I do with you?" the teacher grumbled as he sorted through a pile of music. "Learn this for next week," he said, shoving at Albert the music for Mendelssohn's *Songs Without Words*, opened to no. 1 "Andante con moto in E Major." "I have no doubt you will spoil it for me as you have just done with Mozart. If you have no feeling for music, I cannot put it in you."

Walking home after the lesson, Albert was stung by Herr Munch's words. "If you have no feeling for music . . . !" For most of Albert's life, music had been one of his greatest pleasures. There and then Albert decided to show his music teacher that his assessment of him was wrong. He had a deep feeling for music, Eugène Munch would see. Throughout the week Albert diligently practiced. Over and over he worked on it until he knew he was playing with feeling and passion. His efforts paid off.

As Albert sat down at the piano to play, Herr Munch asked him, "Are you about to spoil Mendelssohn for me?" His words rolled off Albert, who placed his hands on the piano keys and began playing. When Albert had finished, Herr Munch walked over to him, placed his hands on Albert's shoulders, and simply said, "Thank you." Albert felt a chill run down his spine. He'd done it. He had proved he did have a feeling for music. From then on Albert focused hard on playing music with feeling, and he and Herr Munch became close friends.

In 1890 Albert turned fifteen, the age at which all Lutheran children were confirmed into the Lutheran Church. Albert found the confirmation classes conducted by Pastor Wennagel difficult to relate to. He felt the pastor gave simplistic answers to difficult questions regarding faith. Nonetheless, on Palm Sunday Albert joined the group of young people walking in a processional from the church vestry to the altar. The morning sun beamed through the vivid stained-glass windows, and Albert's heart was full as he heard the sound of the organ grow louder. Herr Munch was playing one of his favorite hymns, "Lift Up Your Heads, O Ye Gates." It was a stirring moment that Albert knew he would always remember.

Many things changed following confirmation. One of the most important, as far as Albert was concerned, was that Herr Munch suggested it was time for him to begin playing the church organ. Excitement pulsed through Albert the first time he climbed the stairs into the organ loft of St. Stephen's Church. The organ was magnificent. Albert slid onto the bench in front of the manuals and stared at them. What sounds those keys made in the hands of a gifted organist like Herr Munch! Before long, his teacher assured him, Albert would be playing Bach's stirring music on the organ. Albert could hardly wait.

Things also were looking up back in Gunsbach. Albert's family moved into a new, much larger manse, a gift from the son of the church's previous pastor. Sunlight streamed in through the many windows. With all the sunlight, Albert's father's health began to improve. About the same time, a distant relative of Albert's mother died and left her an inheritance. It wasn't enough to make the family rich, but it certainly meant that his mother was less concerned about money than she had been for years.

Despite the family's extra income, Albert didn't want to ask his parents for money to buy something he really wanted—his own bicycle. Instead, he set about earning it himself. Although he'd found mathematics particularly difficult, Albert had applied himself to the subject and was now near the top of his class. He decided to tutor younger students in math and save the money he earned for a bicycle.

By now, Albert had found a rhythm to his studies. He had to work hard at most subjects but now consistently got good grades. In August 1893, he passed his final written and oral tests. His years of studying at the gymnasium in Mulhouse were behind him, and Albert was eager to start at the University of Strasbourg in the fall. In the meantime, he headed back to Gunsbach to visit his family.

At the beginning of October 1893, a month before Albert was due to start his studies in philosophy and theology at the University of Strasbourg, he was sitting on a Paris-bound train. The trip was a surprising turn of events for him. Following graduation from the gymnasium at Mulhouse, his father's two oldest brothers, Uncle Charles and Uncle Auguste, had sent Albert a train ticket to come visit them in Paris, where they lived. Albert had never been to Paris before, and there was a lot he wanted to see and do in the city.

Uncle Charles, a high school German teacher, met Albert at the Paris train station. Together they caught a fiacre, or horse-drawn cab. As the horse clopped along, several automobiles passed the fiacre in both directions. "It's getting to be a problem," Uncle Charles told Albert. "There are so many automobiles on the road now, and they go wherever they want, cutting off horses and scaring cyclists. Thank goodness the city is doing something about it. Look," he said, pointing at one of the passing vehicles. "The Paris police have passed a law that each automobile driving in the city must have a metal plate bearing the owner's name and address on its left side. It's the first law like it in the world, I believe. Maybe that will make them slow down a little. I'm sure one vehicle passed us going ten miles an hour when I came to collect you."

Albert nodded, recalling the first time he had seen a bicycle back in Gunsbach. Now roads were being overrun by another invention—noisy automobiles. The world was certainly moving forward.

Uncle Charles and his wife, Louise, welcomed Albert into their fashionable home in Neuilly-sur-Seine. Albert had met their three children, his cousins, when they had visited Gunsbach. Georges was two months younger than Albert, Emile was sixteen years old, and Anne Marie was eleven. It felt good to be among young people again after having lived alone with Uncle Louis and Aunt Sophie for nearly ten years.

"There are many people to introduce you to," Uncle Charles told Albert. "You'll find Paris an exciting city compared to Gunsbach or even Mulhouse." He laughed, and Albert laughed with him. Albert was already impressed with the size of Paris. Over the next few days, his cousins took him to the Louvre art museum and the recently erected Eiffel Tower, built to be the entrance archway for the 1889 World's Fair. Albert marveled at the tower's height and its latticed wrought-iron structure. The four cousins also went to the enormous department store Le Bon Marché on rue de Sèvres, and they carried on to see the equally large Notre-Dame cathedral. Once inside the church, Albert was anxious to see the pipe organ. It was impressive. Twenty-five years earlier, Aristide Cavaillé-Coll had built the organ using pipework from the former organ it replaced. While the organ was quite a spectacle, Albert knew it wasn't the grandest organ in Paris. Aristide Cavaillé-Coll's masterpiece was the organ in Saint-Sulpice, the second-largest church in Paris after Notre-Dame. In fact, Albert harbored a secret dream of meeting Charles-Marie Widor, organist at Saint-Sulpice, while in Paris. Widor was probably the most famous organist and organ music composer in the world.

Uncle Auguste was a successful and well-connected Parisian businessman. While visiting him and his wife, Mathilde, Albert mentioned his desire to meet Charles Widor. "Well, then, you really must," Aunt Mathilde said. "We have a mutual friend. I will write you a letter of introduction and have it sent to Monsieur Widor today."

Albert could hardly believe his good fortune. A letter of introduction was just what he needed! Throughout the next day he waited nervously to see if Charles Widor would respond. He did, and better yet, he invited Albert to play the grand organ at Saint-Sulpice the following Wednesday. It would be a dream come true, and Albert could hardly wait for the day to arrive.

Chapter 6

A Man of Many Talents

Albert set out mid-morning the following Wednesday for his appointment with Charles-Marie Widor. Getting there proved challenging. Paris residents were celebrating a new alliance between France and Russia. Previously the French had had few alliances with other European countries, and this new alliance made them feel safer, especially from attacks by Germany and the Austro-Hungarians. That morning a street parade was taking place in honor of the agreement, which was known as the Dual Alliance. Russian sailors in crisp, white uniforms marched in the streets along with French soldiers. It seemed to Albert the whole population of Paris was out in the streets celebrating.

Albert pushed through the crowd but made slow progress. By the time he reached Luxembourg Gardens, it was almost time for his appointment. He ran through the gardens to make up for lost time. When he exited at the north end, he jostled his way through two more blocks of people until the imposing structure of the church of Saint-Sulpice towered over him. He headed to the lane at the rear of the church and was soon standing before Charles Widor's door. Albert took a moment to catch his breath before knocking and entering. Charles Widor sat at a grand piano with an attached foot pedal unit mimicking organ pedals, which allowed him to play bass notes with his feet.

"I'm Albert Schweitzer," Albert introduced himself.

Charles stood, walked over to him, and shook Albert's hand. "It's busy out there today."

Albert nodded. "I'm sorry to be running late."

Charles waved his hand. "So, you play the organ, Monsieur Schweitzer? What will you play for me?"

Albert relaxed. "I will play Bach, of course."

"Good. Good," Charles said, leading Albert from his music room into the cavernous, silent nave of Saint-Sulpice. At the back of the nave sat the enormous organ. Albert stopped and stared at it for a moment. "Magnificent," he whispered.

"The most beautiful organ in the world," Charles agreed as the two men climbed into the organ loft. Albert slid onto the organ bench while the master organist sat on a seat to the side. The pipe organ had five manuals and one hundred stops. Albert sat quietly for a few moments before he began to play. Immediately the church filled with swirling chords of music. Albert was transfixed. He shut everything else out, even Charles Widor, and focused solely on playing the chorale prelude. When Albert had finished, Charles stared at him. "How soon can you come to me for lessons?" he asked.

Albert felt a chill run down his spine. The greatest pipe organist in the world was offering him lessons. They worked out a schedule so that for the next three weeks Albert could play the organ at Saint-Sulpice under Charles Widor's direction. Despite there being a thirty-one-year age gap between the two men, they bonded over their love of music. At one lesson Charles said, "You will understand what I mean when I say that to play the organ, your whole will must be filled with a vision of eternity." Albert nodded. He understood exactly.

At the end of the three weeks, Albert left Paris to begin his studies at Strasbourg, where he moved into his tiny rooms at the Theological College of St. Thomas, a branch of the University of Strasbourg. He loved the rooms from the moment he stepped inside. Two large windows looked out over a walled garden. A fringe of poplar trees grew on the bank of the Ill River, which wound its way through the city to the Rhine two miles away. Even though the Rhine flowed north for another 350 miles before reaching the North Sea, Strasbourg was a bustling port filled with fishermen, shipbuilders, quays, and traveling boats.

Albert loved the fact that the city had a long history, reaching back over nineteen hundred years. During that time some significant events had taken place in Strasbourg. In 1440, Johannes Gutenberg developed the first printing press about a mile from where Albert was now living. In 1520, three years after Martin Luther nailed his Ninety-Five Theses to the church door in Wittenberg, setting the Protestant Reformation in motion, Strasbourg became one of the earliest cities to embrace Luther's teaching. John Calvin, the Protestant reformer, preached at the Church of St. Nicholas in 1538. The following year, while still in Strasbourg, Calvin produced the second edition of his *Institutes,* enlarging it from its previous six chapters to seventeen. In fact, just on the other side of the Ill River from the Theological College, sat the church where John Calvin had preached. It was a small, brownstone Gothic structure with a high-pitched roof built over 450 years before. It was the same church where Uncle Albert Schillinger, Albert's mother's brother, had been the pastor.

Albert was glad he'd saved enough money to buy a bicycle while he was a student in Mulhouse. He was able to use the bike to ride the mile over narrow cobblestone streets from St. Thomas to the main university campus, where he attended a lecture every weekday morning at eleven.

Once in Strasbourg, Albert met with the university faculty and set himself an ambitious course load. He would study for a degree in theology and also take classes in music theory and philosophy.

Albert did one other thing before settling into university life. He rode to St. William's Church with a letter of introduction to Ernst Munch from his brother Eugène. The brothers were both excellent organists, and Albert hoped that Ernst would take him on as a student. He was not disappointed. Ernst welcomed him warmly. He'd already heard from his brother in Mulhouse and had been waiting for Albert to arrive. Albert was excited when he learned that Ernst, who was the choir director at St. William's and taught organ at the Strasbourg Conservatory, was looking for a new choir organist. He offered Albert the position, which Albert gladly accepted.

St. William's was several blocks from the university campus. Albert loved everything about the church. It was built as a monastery in the fourteenth century by a knight who had returned home to Strasbourg unharmed from the Crusades. The church's nave had high ceilings that provided excellent acoustics and housed a wonderful pipe organ that produced notes that were crisp and clear.

Albert felt an immediate connection with Ernst Munch. Although Ernst was fifteen years older than Albert and had a wife and six young children, the two men spent hours together making plans to hold Bach concerts at St. William's. Whenever Albert was able to fit it in, he made short trips to Paris to take more lessons from Charles Widor.

In April 1894 Albert's life in Strasbourg was interrupted when he was called up for a year of compulsory military training in the German army.

At nineteen years of age, he was drafted into the army's 143rd Regiment. Albert moved into a barracks outside of town along with about a hundred other young men the same age, most of them farmers' sons from the surrounding countryside. Albert was resigned to the training, except for losing a year of study at the university. However, an army captain took pity on him and gave Albert permission to attend his morning lectures, as long as all his army duties were completed on time. Albert was delighted. Each weekday morning after drills in the barracks square, he bicycled into the old city and listened to the lectures before pedaling back to training camp. In the evenings, while the other soldiers passed their time playing cards or telling jokes, Albert studied his pocket-sized Greek New Testament.

Although none of his fellow trainee soldiers were studying, they didn't tease him because of his study habits. Albert supposed that because of his height (over six feet tall) and his physical strength in manning ropes and dragging gun carriages through muddy ditches, he'd already proven himself.

In mid-April 1895, Albert's year of military training was over. He returned to the Theological College of St. Thomas in top physical condition and with a clear idea of what he particularly wanted to study. During hundreds of hours reading the Greek New Testament, he'd become fascinated with the different accounts of Jesus's life recorded in the Synoptic Gospels (the first three books of the New Testament). His reading left him with many questions: Which Gospel was the first one to be written? Which Gospels had been written using that first one as a source? Why did the Gospel of Matthew include things Jesus said that didn't appear in the other Gospels? And how did that change the way Christianity developed?

Now that Albert had a focus for his studies, he worked harder than ever. In the spring of 1896, Uncle Auguste and Aunt Mathilde sent him a ticket to a concert in the Bavarian town of Bayreuth, where the famous German composer Richard Wagner had built a large concert hall. Although Wagner had died thirteen years before, his widow, Cosima, kept his memory alive with an annual concert in his honor. The concert had grown to be one of the most renowned musical events in all Germany. Albert knew he was lucky to have a ticket, except he had no money to buy a train ticket for the nine-hour trip to Bayreuth. Because missing the concert was out of the question, Albert cut his food budget from three meals a day to one until he'd saved the money for the train fare.

As soon as he arrived in Bayreuth, Albert knew his visit would be worth the sacrifice. It was amazing to be in the presence of so many others who shared the same passion for music as he did.

On the way home, Albert stopped in Stuttgart, Germany, to see the new pipe organ recently installed in the Liederhalle, where he was given permission to play the organ. Albert was shocked to discover it was the worst pipe organ he'd ever played. The notes sounded jangly and indistinct. *How,* he asked himself, *would anyone think this new modern organ was better than the old handcrafted ones Europe's greatest composers had played on?*

Albert left Stuttgart deeply troubled. If pastors and town leaders continued replacing grand old pipe organs with these inferior-sounding modern instruments, soon there would be no place to go to hear the music of Bach or Wagner the way it was meant to be heard. By the time he got off the train in Strasbourg, Albert was determined to do something about the situation. In addition to his theology, philosophy, and music studies, he would study how classical pipe organs were built and learn how to preserve them. The daunting task involved visiting small churches in the German and French countryside and urging pastors to restore their organs rather than getting rid of them as the instruments aged. As his studies progressed, Albert soon knew enough that he could repair organs himself.

Over the summer of 1896, twenty-one-year-old Albert was ready for a rest. He rode the train to Gunsbach to spend two months with his family. He found his parents in good health and spirits and his younger brother and sisters happy. Although he loved Strasbourg, Albert was glad to be back in the village. He helped his father in the garden, played the church organ, and took the church youth group on several day excursions into the mountains. He also went to Colmar to visit his oldest sister, Louisa, who had recently married Jules Ehrtsmann.

Walking through Colmar's streets, Albert could see versions of his life stretch out before him. He could become a country pastor like his father, with a wife and children running around the manse. He could become a concert organist and make a name for himself as an expert on Bach. Or he could work his way into a full-time college professorship. In addition to his doctorate studies in theology, his philosophy professor, Dr. Ziegler, also had him hard at work on a second doctorate in philosophy. All these career paths were exciting possibilities. It was just a matter of deciding which one to follow. Or was it? Something deep inside Albert bothered him. He had so many good career options to choose. But what if that wasn't what God wanted for him? What if God had a different plan for his life?

As he thought about this, the statue of the African man he'd seen as a child in the Champ de Mars memorial garden flashed through his mind. He walked to the garden and viewed the statue once more. Staring at it, he had the strangest feeling he was supposed to do something to help people in Africa.

One morning back in Gunsbach, as Albert opened a window and looked out over the fruit trees, he felt moved to make God a promise. He would pursue music, philosophy, theology, and organ building for nine more years, until he was thirty. At that time, he would stop whatever he was doing and spend the rest of his life serving God in whatever form God showed him. Albert latched the window and bounded downstairs. He felt more alive than he had in a long time. His mother smiled as he sat down for breakfast. He started to tell her about his decision, then held back.

This was a private decision, Albert told himself. *No one else needs to know about it until it's time for action.*

Albert's vacation was soon over, and he returned to Strasbourg, where he threw himself into his studies. He also found time to play the organ at St. William's Church for choral concerts that Ernst Munch organized, and on Sundays he often preached at the Church of St. Nicholas. He also continued studying how to repair and preserve pipe organs.

During the second half of 1897, Albert began work on the thesis for his theology degree. It was titled "The Idea of the Last Supper in Daniel Schleiermacher, Compared with the Ideas of Luther, Zwingli and Calvin." In early 1898, he completed the thesis, and on May 6, twenty-three-year old Albert successfully defended it, earning his doctorate degree in theology.

Soon after defending his thesis and earning his theology degree, Albert attended the wedding of Lina Haas and Willibald Conrad. The Schweitzer and Haas families had known each other for years. At the wedding, Albert sat next to a young woman who introduced herself as Hélène Bresslau. Albert recognized her as a member of St. William's choir, though he'd never spoken to her. The two soon struck up a conversation. Albert learned that Hélène's father, Harry, was a history professor at the university and that she was a music student at the Strasbourg Conservatory. Along with her two brothers and parents, Hélène had spent her childhood in Berlin.

By end of the wedding Hélène and Albert were getting along nicely. She belonged to a bicycle club and invited Albert to join. Albert loved riding his bicycle and thought he might enjoy taking long rides out into the countryside with the club members. He and Hélène soon discovered that they had a large circle of friends in common. Albert also met Hélène's older brother, Ernst, who was studying medicine and zoology at the university. As they got to know each other, Albert learned that Hélène was born to Jewish parents, but her father had insisted the family convert to Lutheranism when she was seven years old in response to the growing anti-Jewish faction in Germany.

Later that year, Albert left to study philosophy at Sorbonne University in Paris, which meant he could once more take organ lessons from Charles Widor. When he wasn't taking lessons, he was studying, often staying up all night. Albert was young, fit, and in a hurry to absorb as much knowledge as possible, in this case about Immanuel Kant. He spent hours in the library, reading volume after volume of the German philosopher's writing and taking notes before starting to write his thesis, titled "The Religious Philosophy of Kant." When Albert did find extra time in his hectic schedule, he visited villages whose churches had pipe organs, recommending repairs and cataloging all he saw.

Albert continued to find his lessons with Charles Widor invigorating. During the lessons, the two men had deep discussions about various composers, particularly Bach. During one such conversation, Charles commented on how strange some of Bach's arrangements were. The music had sudden mood changes not usually found in choral preludes, and Bach would pass quickly from one musical idea to another. Albert was surprised when he learned that his teacher had been playing Bach's music all this time yet didn't realize that these sudden changes were where Bach had woven Lutheran hymn melodies into his compositions.

Johann Sebastian Bach was a German Lutheran, and in his compositions, he paid homage to the hymns that had shaped him in his youth. Having grown up Lutheran, Albert naturally recognized many classic Lutheran hymns in the pieces Bach wrote. Albert played some of these musical passages for Charles, explaining the hymns and their words. He chuckled to himself at the look on his teacher's face. Charles seemed astonished at how simple the answer was. "You must write a paper about this," he told Albert. "We French organists are Catholic. We have no idea about this aspect of Bach's work. You must inform us." With a smile, Albert dutifully added this to his list of things to do. But first he had to finish his thesis.

Through hard work and natural intelligence, Albert completed his thesis on Immanuel Kant and returned to Strasbourg. He successfully defended his thesis and was awarded his degree. At age twenty-four, he now held doctorate degrees in theology and philosophy. But Albert still had one more year of study ahead of him to get his licentiate in theology, which would allow him to become a licensed Lutheran pastor. He received his licentiate later that year, just in time for the start of the twentieth century.

Albert's days of formal study were now behind him, and he began preparing to take up a position as youth pastor at St. Nicholas Church in Strasbourg, where he had occasionally preached as a student. When people asked him if he had other ambitions, Albert would just smile. He was still five years away from turning thirty, and he was confident that everything would change at that time. He just didn't yet know how.

Chapter 7

A Peace Settled over Him

Five years rolled by quickly, and when Albert turned thirty in 1905, he was well known around Strasbourg and throughout much of France and Germany. He already had two books published. One was his thesis on Immanuel Kant. The other was *J. S. Bach, Le Musicien-Poète,* the result of Charles Widor's suggestion. Albert had also finished writing two other manuscripts for publication. The first contained all he'd learned about the repair, maintenance, and care of pipe organs. The second was titled *The Quest of the Historical Jesus.* This manuscript had grown from Albert's reading and study of the Synoptic Gospels in Greek during his year of conscription in the German army ten years before. He had also written numerous university papers in the fields of music, religion, and philosophy. An acclaimed organist and world authority on Bach, Albert also served as a pastor at St. Nicholas Church in Strasbourg and was now principal of the Theological College of St. Thomas.

In the seven years since meeting Hélène Bresslau, Albert had stayed in close contact with her through letters. Albert enjoyed telling Hélène all he was doing, and he was interested in learning about her accomplishments. Hélène had completed courses in medieval and modern history at the University of Strasbourg and had spent six months in Italy. This was followed by three months in England teaching English, French, and music at a girls' school in Brighton. While in England, Hélène wrote Albert about how she was also studying the orphan-care work of Dr. Thomas Barnardo and how inspired she was by all she was learning. As a result, Hélène was now studying to become the first female inspector of orphans for the city of Strasbourg.

One morning in 1905, while sitting at his desk at the Theological College correcting student papers, Albert noticed the green cover of a magazine. Since he didn't recall having seen it before, he reached over and picked the magazine up. It turned out to be the latest edition of the Paris Evangelical Missionary Society's magazine. Albert smiled thinking of his childhood and the Sunday afternoons he had spent listening to his father read missionary letters printed in the magazine.

Through the years Albert had maintained an interest in Africa and had read a lot about its struggles.

For a long time, inland Africa had remained a mysterious and unexplored place for Europeans, but from 1850 on, a steady march of European explorers, including Henry Stanley, Pierre de Brazza, Sir Richard Burton, and David Livingstone, made their way inland by following the navigable rivers. None of the European empires wanted to miss out on the biggest land grab in the world that could yield untold natural resources such as rubber, ivory, gold, silver, tin, hardwoods, and perhaps even diamonds. With sailing ships giving way to new steam-powered vessels, Europeans needed refueling ports of call around the coast of Africa. Albert was aware that African people were suffering great losses as the colonial powers of Belgium, Great Britain, France, Germany, Italy, Portugal, and Spain fought and bartered for land on the continent. By now, France controlled a huge swath of central and western Africa, which they called French West Africa and French Equatorial Africa. This included parts of the Congo and an area known as Gabon that was nestled on Africa's west coast. France also controlled the island of Madagascar off the east coast of Africa. Germany controlled the area known as Togoland in western Africa, as well as Cameroon and two other colonies: German East Africa and German South-West Africa.

As he thought about Africa, Albert recalled reading how famous explorer Pierre de Brazza had recently returned to French Equatorial Africa to assess how badly things were going for the native population there. The French government had divided much of their African territory among thirty French companies, allowing each company to rule its workforce in whatever way it pleased and to take anything of value from the land. Brazza wanted to see firsthand the impact this exploitation was having on the local people.

Reading through an article in the missionary magazine on the needs of the Congo area, Albert discovered conditions there mirrored what de Brazza was reporting. Many villages in the Congo and Gabon areas had been decimated as able-bodied men were enticed to leave their homes to cut down trees and clear land for foreigners. These men were paid in rum, and many never returned to take up their traditional roles as leaders in their villages.

The article also highlighted the needs of a tiny mission station at a place called Lambaréné on the banks of the Ogowe River in Gabon. The mission station was situated forty-seven miles south of the equator and roughly one hundred miles inland from the coast. A small school was held there, but a medical clinic was desperately needed, since there was no doctor within a hundred-mile radius. The local people had nowhere to turn when their bodies were ravaged by such diseases as leprosy, sleeping sickness, malaria, and tuberculosis.

The Reverend Alfred Boegner, author of the article, ended by stating, "I hope that those on whom the Master's eyes have already rested will answer the call . . . . There are men and women who can reply simply to the Master's call, 'Lord, I am coming' . . . . Those are the people whom the Church needs."

When he had finished reading, Albert sat quietly. A peace settled over him. He was now thirty years old, and true to his promise, he was searching for a way to serve God for the rest of his life. He remembered Jesus's instructions to His disciples to go into all the world to preach the word, heal the sick, and cast out evil spirits. "Remember," Jesus had admonished, "freely you have received, freely give" (Matthew 10:8). Albert was immediately struck by how much he'd been given. Was it too much for Jesus Christ to ask him to help the people he'd just read about in their need? No, he concluded, it was not. Albert was sure that God was calling him to work alongside the Paris Evangelical Missionary Society as a medical doctor in Lambaréné.

Albert told no one about his new plan except Hélène. He knew she would understand his need to put Christian words into action. With little fanfare, Albert set about preparing to go back to university once more—this time to study medicine for six years. He wrote a long letter to Alfred Boegner, author of the article and director of the Paris Evangelical Missionary Society, offering his services as soon as he finished his medical training. He concluded by saying,

> I have grown increasingly simpler, and more and more childlike, and have come to realize more and more clearly that the sole truth and sole happiness consist in serving our Lord Jesus Christ wherever he needs us. I have mulled it over hundreds of times; I have

> meditated. Absorbed in my thoughts about Jesus, I have asked myself whether I could live without scholarship, without art, without the intellectual environment in which I now exist—and all my reflections have always ended with a joyous "Yes."

During this time, as Albert shifted his thinking toward becoming a missionary doctor and began counting the cost, Pierre de Brazza died in Africa of either dysentery or poisoning. His body was shipped to Paris, where he received a state funeral. In the aftermath of the explorer's death, it seemed to Albert that every newspaper in France carried articles examining the difficulties Europeans faced trying to survive the harsh environment of Equatorial Africa. Nine months after the death of Brazza, newspaper headlines announced the death of George Grenfell, a famous Cornish missionary and explorer who had lived in the Congo and succumbed to blackwater fever. Yet while these prominent deaths in Equatorial Africa deterred some, they spurred Albert on.

One year after making the decision to go to Africa as a medical missionary, Albert decided it was time to tell everyone the news. By now he had enrolled in medical school at Strasbourg University, where he would begin his course of study in the fall. On Saturday, October 13, 1906, while staying with his uncle and aunt in Paris, Albert sat down and wrote letters to his family, close friends, and employer. Albert then walked to the postbox on Avenue de le Grande Armée. As he dropped in the letters, he realized it was one thing to write them but quite another to actually mail them. He thought about the consequences of what he'd just done. He was sure that most of those who opened their letter would be shocked and unable to comprehend his decision. He hoped that a few would stand with him in his decision, as Hélène was doing.

Responses to the letters were swift, and harsher than Albert expected. The letters offered a variety of advice: "Stay where your roots are." "If you don't think you are receiving enough recognition for your work, be patient, it will come!" "You can do more good by staying here, lecturing, and playing the organ—you could do charity concerts and send the proceeds to the mission in Africa. You don't have to go there yourself." One letter contained the dire warning, "You will be dead within five years if you go to live on the equator!"

Some responses stung more than others. Organist Charles Widor was appalled that Albert would consider such a move. "You are like a general who exposes himself like a common soldier on the front line," he wrote.

Albert was most shocked, however, by his parents' response when he saw them in person a week later. He explained to his father that while he loved being a teacher of theology and a preacher, he now felt it was time to stop talking about his faith and put it into action on the mission field. Louis Schweitzer begged his son to reconsider, reminding him that

French Equatorial Africa was one of the deadliest places in the world for a white person to live. Albert found his father's attitude hard to reconcile with the sermons he preached about missions many Sunday afternoons at church. He hoped his father would come to understand.

Back in Strasbourg, Albert settled into student life at the same university at which he'd been a professor and principal of the theological college. It seemed a little odd at first, especially since his fellow students had come straight from high school, and Albert knew they thought of him as an old man. As he began studying chemistry, bacteriology, and pharmacology at medical school, Albert realized his memory wasn't as good as it had been in his early twenties. It would take a lot of work to keep up with the class.

Albert had some savings set aside, and he accepted a few organ recital bookings in Paris and Munich to help him keep afloat financially. In addition, the university asked him to stay on as a lecturer for several months while a suitable replacement was found for him. Albert happily obliged.

Albert's friendship with Hélène continued, though the two didn't spend a lot of time together. On one occasion Hélène made a trip to London, where she heard a lecture by Dr. Henry Grattan Guinness, a British missionary trainer. He spoke about the terrible human rights abuses taking place in the Belgian Congo. When she returned to Strasbourg, she began relating to Albert the many horrible things Dr. Guinness had spoken of. As Albert listened quietly, the more certain he became that he was called to do something practical about the human suffering European empire building was inflicting upon the African people.

Albert was used to a busy life and now drove himself as never before. On top of his medical studies and continuing to give theology lectures, he preached almost every Sunday at St. Nicholas Church and played the organ at the Bach Society concert in Paris every winter as well as at other concerts in France, Spain, and Germany.

While Albert kept busy, Hélène and her friend Elly Knapp opened a new home for unwed mothers and their babies in Strasbourg. The first of its kind in Germany, it was modeled after the work of Dr. Thomas Barnardo in England. Albert helped out whenever he could.

As his studies progressed, Albert was faced with the question of whether to go to Africa as a single missionary or marry Hélène and go as a couple. The decision was made more difficult every time he read a newsletter from the Paris Evangelical Missionary Society. Missionaries in Africa were dying from blackwater fever and malaria. In just two years the mission had experienced the deaths of two male and three female missionaries. It was sobering to think of asking Hélène to marry him and follow him to such a dangerous area. Yet as he prayed about it, Albert felt it was the right thing to do. He would ask and then rely on her to decide whether or not it was her calling. On the train back to Strasbourg after a visit to Gunsbach, Albert asked Hélène to marry him. To his surprise she quickly agreed, though they both decided to keep their engagement secret until after Albert finished medical school and his residency in early 1913.

Now that they were engaged, Hélène talked to Albert about how she could prepare for a life of service in Equatorial Africa. In the end she decided to return to school to become a nurse. In this way Hélène could assist Albert in surgeries and take on many of the responsibilities of running a clinic or hospital. Leaving her job supervising orphans in Strasbourg, Hélène moved to Frankfurt and enrolled in a rigorous one-year nursing program.

In September 1910, Hélène graduated from the nurses training school, but she was not well. Albert was alarmed to learn she had a small, painful tumor on her spine. After leaving the training school, Hélène headed for a sanatorium in the Black Forest to rest. She returned to Strasbourg in early 1911 feeling much better.

In June 1911, Albert attended the wedding of his brother Paul to Emma Munch at St. William's Church. Albert was delighted. Emma was the daughter of Ernst Munch and the niece of Eugène Munch, Albert's old music teacher in Mulhouse. At the wedding, Albert tried to avoid talking about politics, despite some troubling developments. The Germans had just dispatched a gunboat, the SMS *Panther*, to the Moroccan port of Agadir to challenge French troops fighting a rebellion there against the ruling sultan. Many Germans felt that France was gaining too much influence in Europe and North Africa and that their government should be as equally aggressive. Albert wasn't sure where all this would end, but he didn't like the direction in which things were going.

Meanwhile, Albert learned that the board of the Paris Evangelical Missionary Society had met several times to discuss his proposal to join them. They had not reached a decision, and more meetings were planned. Their concerns had to do with the fact that Albert was a German wanting to join a French organization at a time of rising political tension between the two countries.

At Christmas in 1911, Albert and Hélène officially announced their engagement. Six months later, on June 18, 1912, wedding bells rang out over Gunsbach as Albert and Hélène were married. Albert was thirty-seven years old, and Hélène was thirty-three. They had already become a strong and determined team, and everyone at the wedding knew they had set their sights on serving as missionaries at Lambaréné in French Equatorial Africa. But before any of that could happen, Albert still had to complete his medical degree and convince the Paris Evangelical Missionary Society to accept him.

Chapter 8

Setting Foot in Africa

Following a short honeymoon, Albert returned to his medical studies to fulfill the final requirements for his degree. He traveled to Paris and studied tropical diseases. While there he met individually with board members of the Paris Evangelical Missionary Society. Some meetings went better than others. A number of the society's board members were suspicious of Albert's motives. They asked if he wanted to confuse Africans with the deep theological principles laid out in his books, particularly *The Quest of the Historical Jesus,* instead of sticking to basic Bible teachings on sin and salvation. Albert assured them he had no intention of confusing anyone, going so far as promising not to preach at all in Africa, confining himself solely to practicing medicine.

At last Albert and the board reached an agreement. He would not preach in Africa, he would use his book royalties to support himself and Hélène while there, and he would take full responsibility for raising funds to equip and run the hospital. Albert estimated the equipment would cost around 25,000 French francs, plus another 1,500 francs a month to keep the hospital running. In return, the Paris Evangelical Missionary Society would allot Albert land, build a simple corrugated ironclad hospital at Lambaréné, provide him and Hélène a house to live in, and promote his work in the mission society's magazine.

Once the agreement had been reached, Albert and Hélène set to work collecting equipment, medicines, and everything else they would need to outfit the new hospital at Lambaréné. At first Albert found this a tedious chore, but as he and Hélène tackled the challenge together, he began to appreciate checking items off his long list as they came in. One by one they packed items into old tea chests and stenciled on the side of them the monogram "ASB" for Albert Schweitzer Bresslau.

Albert and Hélène tried to visit Gunsbach as often as they could, but Albert's mother couldn't adjust to the idea of his giving up everything to go to Africa, where she believed he would most likely die. She would sit tight-lipped whenever he talked about the future.

Thankfully Albert had many things to do that diverted him from his mother's gloomy predictions.

He crisscrossed Germany and France, describing his vision for a hospital in Africa and collecting money and other donations for it. He also gave many pipe organ recitals to raise money.

To Albert's delight, one of his professors donated most of the medical equipment needed. Albert was particularly grateful for this, since the professor was a German donating to a French mission undertaking. Albert also packed over one hundred of his books, hoping to find time in Africa to continue studying and writing.

In early February 1913, Albert Schweitzer passed his final practical surgical exam and was awarded his doctorate in medicine. He was jubilant. It had taken him six exhausting years, but he'd done it. Now he and Hélène could begin their final preparations for Africa.

A month later, on March 9, 1913, Albert preached a farewell sermon at the Church of St. Nicholas in Strasbourg. As the text for his sermon he chose Philippians 4:7: "The peace of God, which passes all understanding, shall keep your hearts and minds in Christ Jesus." Albert went on to explain that the peace of God is like the distant snow-covered peaks of a mountain range which gleam in the sun as they rise above the mist. Hidden in the mist are foothills, which everyone who wishes to reach the peaks must climb. Many people are happy to live in the mist and not concern themselves with reaching the peaks, but the Christian life requires us to keep reaching higher and accepting new challenges.

Buoyed by the best wishes of the congregation members in Strasbourg, Albert and Hélène traveled on to Gunsbach, where Albert gave a farewell sermon to his family and friends on March 16. This service was an emotional ordeal for Albert, especially because his mother barely spoke to him. Although Albert wished he could reassure her that everything would turn out fine, he realized he couldn't guarantee that.

On the morning of Good Friday, March 21, 1913, it was time for Albert to say goodbye to his family. His mother stood by mutely as he and Hélène hugged everyone around them and climbed aboard the train for Strasbourg. In Strasbourg the couple spent a night with Hélène's parents and caught the train to Paris the following day. Upon arrival in Paris, they enjoyed Charles-Marie Widor's Easter organ recital at Saint-Sulpice.

At the recital Albert learned that the Bach Society of Paris had a gift for him. They had ordered a specially built piano as a thank-you for his long years of service to the music of J.S. Bach. The interior of the three-ton upright piano was encased in zinc to help it withstand the tropical climate of Africa. The instrument was also fitted with organ pedals instead of the normal piano pedals, so that Albert could keep up his footwork practice in Africa. The new piano was waiting for him in Bordeaux. Albert was touched by the thoughtfulness of the gesture, though he doubted he would have the time or energy to continue his music in Africa. That was something he'd already come to terms with. However, just in case he did have the time, Albert had packed five hundred music manuscripts to take with him.

Following the recital in Paris, the Schweitzers caught another train for the 350-mile trip south to Bordeaux. There they collected seventy crates of equipment for the new hospital that had been sent on ahead. The crates, the new piano, and all their other baggage had to clear customs before being loaded onto the steamer *Europe*, which was docked at Pauillac in La Gironde Estuary, a few miles downriver from Bordeaux.

March 26, 1913, was a sunny day with the promise of spring in the air. Hélène and Albert stood together on the deck of the *Europe* as it left the estuary and sailed out into the Bay of Biscay.

Albert had traveled around France, Germany, and several other European countries by train and sometimes on his bicycle, but he'd never sailed on a ship before. At first, he found the movement of the *Europe* beneath his feet a little disconcerting. Not only did the vessel roll from side to side between port and starboard, but also it pitched back and forth from bow to stern with the motion of the ocean currents. It reminded Albert of the rocking horse he had had as a child. By evening he felt he was getting used to the ship's motion, and he accompanied Hélène to the dining salon, where they ate dinner with the other three hundred passengers.

As they readied for bed that night, Albert noticed that the *Europe* was beginning to pitch and roll more and more violently. Soon after he and Hélène had crawled into their bunks, the two trunks stowed in their cabin began sliding across the cabin and crashing into the bulkheads. Albert climbed from his bunk to secure the trunks, but his timing was wrong. One of the trunks came hurtling toward him, and he had to dive back into his bunk for safety. Albert and Hélène spent the rest of the night listening to the sliding and banging of their trunks. As he lay there, Albert thought of the seventy crates of equipment in the ship's hold. Were they tied down well enough to stay in place in the turbulent swells? And the piano—what damage would it suffer if it came loose and started rolling about?

In the morning the steward came to the cabin to check on the couple. He showed Albert the correct way to tie down the trunks so they wouldn't have to endure another night like that. Albert listened with interest as the steward explained that ships like the *Europe* that plied the African coast were known as Congo boats. They had shallow drafts that allowed them to enter sandy harbors and river estuaries. But the shallow drafts also caused them to pitch and roll at sea much more than other ships, especially in the heavy swells they were currently experiencing.

The steward informed Albert and Hélène that things aboard were probably going to get a lot worse, as the ship appeared to be headed into a storm. His prediction proved correct. For the next three days the ship was lashed by fierce wind and rain. The *Europe* pitched and rolled so violently that the cooks couldn't prepare meals in the galley. Because it was also too dangerous for passengers to move about the vessel, Albert and Hélène stayed safely in their cabin.

The storm abated shortly before the *Europe* reached Tenerife in the Canary Islands, two hundred miles off the western coast of North Africa. By the time Albert made it out on deck, two barges had been tied up alongside the ship, and coal was being loaded into the *Europe's* bunkers to fire the boilers. Albert checked on the state of things in the hold. He was relieved to discover that the piano and all the crates were still securely lashed down.

By mid-afternoon the coal bunkers had been filled, and more food supplies had been taken aboard. The captain then gave the order to weigh anchor, and the *Europe* steamed away from Tenerife, headed south.

The next day most of those aboard began wearing pith helmets whenever they went outside. When one of the ship's officers saw that Albert and Hélène were not wearing their helmets, he took Albert aside. "Even though the weather is not hot yet," he told him, "from today on, you must regard the sun as your worst enemy, whether it is rising, high in the sky, or setting, and even if it is cloudy. Take it from me, many people get dangerous sunstroke before they even get close to the equator. You must wear your helmet outdoors to help protect yourself from this enemy." Albert unpacked his pith helmet and wore it whenever he was above deck.

With the storm of the first few days behind them, the passengers got to know each other. Albert discovered that most of the other passengers were either army officers, doctors, or civil service officials traveling to France's African colonies. From them Albert gleaned helpful information about the hardships and challenges of living in Africa. One of the most helpful people was a military doctor with twelve years' experience. He was on his way to become director of the Bacteriological Institute in Grand Bassam on the Ivory Coast. After an initial conversation, he agreed to meet with Albert for two hours each morning and give him a thorough and practical understanding of the tropical diseases he would encounter, along with the latest practices for treating them. Albert was grateful for this extra schooling.

After steaming south for a thousand miles, the *Europe* arrived off Dakar, Senegal, which was part of French West Africa. When the ship docked, Albert and Hélène went ashore. At the bottom of the gangplank, Albert paused and took a deep breath before setting foot in Africa for the first time. He and Hélène were now standing together on the continent where they'd pledged to serve God. The weather was hot and humid, and Albert's forehead was covered with beads of sweat, which he dabbed with a large handkerchief pulled from the pocket of his white pants.

From the harbor's edge, the city spread steeply upwards. As they made their way through the bustle of people carrying all manner of packages and baskets, Albert and Hélène reached some market stalls.

Albert recognized some of the fruits and vegetables for sale, but there were other items he'd never seen before.

During their excursion, Albert and Hélène followed one of the streets up a hill. As he rounded a corner, Albert was confronted by an overloaded donkey cart stuck axle-deep in mud. Two African men sat atop the cart, whipping and yelling at the bedraggled donkeys to pull harder. Albert's mind flashed back to the mistreated horse he had seen when he was a small boy visiting his aunt in Colmar. Now here he was in Africa, his new home, witnessing the same cruelty toward animals.

Albert couldn't hold his peace. He could not stand to see the two men abuse the donkeys a moment longer. He yelled at them to climb down from the cart. At first the African men seemed unsure what to do, but eventually they climbed down. Albert got behind the cart and motioned for them to join him. The three men pushed the cart free of the mud. As he walked away, Albert was sure this wouldn't be the last case of animal cruelty he would witness.

From Dakar, the *Europe* made its way to Conakry in Guinea. As it sailed on from there, the ship was now almost always within sight of the coast. When he wasn't reading or writing letters, Albert stood on deck and studied the coastline as it slipped by. He was surprised by the jungle's vivid shades of green. And when he studied the coastline through a telescope, he could see the pointed roofs of African huts and smoke rising from cooking fires.

At each port where the ship stopped, it was time to bid farewell to some new friends they'd made on the journey from France. Each time, Albert wondered whether he would ever see those people again, or whether one of the many dangers of living in Africa would claim their lives.

Early on April 13, 1913, the *Europe* reached Libreville, a thriving city on the coast of Gabon in French Equatorial Africa. From Libreville the ship sailed on to Cape Lopez, eight hours away. On Monday, April 14, it was Albert and Hélène's turn to disembark the *Europe*. The first leg of their journey to Lambaréné was over. As their personal luggage, the seventy crates, and the piano were unloaded onto the dock, Albert was apprehensive. On the journey down he'd heard many tales of how customs officers overcharged and mistreated arriving passengers. He need not have worried. The customs officer treated him and Hélène fairly. Albert breathed a sigh of relief.

Early the next morning, Albert and Hélène boarded the steamer *Alémbé,* a broad, shallow-drafted riverboat with two paddle wheels set side by side at her stern. It was time to start the trip up the Ogowe River to Lambaréné.

Chapter 9

Lambaréné at Last

On April 15, 1913, Albert wrote,

> River and forest . . . ! Who can describe the first impression they make? . . . It is impossible to say where the river ends and the land begins, for a mighty network of roots, clothed with bright-flowering creepers, projects right into the water. Clumps of palms and palm trees, ordinary trees spreading out widely with green boughs and huge leaves, single trees of the pine family shooting up to a towering height between them, wide fields of papyrus clumps as tall as a man, with big fan-like leaves, and amid all this luxuriant greenery the rotting stems of dead giants shooting

> up to heaven. . . . In every gap in the forest a water mirror meets the eye; at every bend in the river a new tributary shows itself. . . . So it goes on hour by hour. . . . Always the same forest and the same yellow water. . . . You shut your eyes for an hour, and when you open them you see exactly what you saw before!

As Albert wrote, he and Hélène sat on the deck of the *Alémbé* as the steamer plied the waters of the Ogowe River between its delta and Ndjolé. About 150 miles upstream, Ndjolé was the last navigable point of the massive river.

Albert caught his wife's eye and smiled. Hélène wore all-white clothing and a pith helmet, as did he. They were getting used to seeing each other dressed in tropical garb. It felt to Albert more like wearing a costume than regular clothes. Going back to his writing, he noted,

> A heron flies heavily up and then settles on a dead tree trunk; white and blue birds skim over the water, and high in the air a pair of ospreys circle. Then—yes, there can be no mistake about it!—from the branch of a palm there hang and swing—two monkey tails! . . . We are really in Africa!

It was true, and Albert put down his pen a moment to ruminate. At last, eight years after reading about the need for doctors in French Equatorial Africa, he was here—with a medical degree and ready to serve. He was aware that the death rate among white missionaries in this region was about 15 percent per year, but he'd made his decision and was at peace with whatever the outcome might be.

Continuing to write, Albert was glad the carbon copy book he had purchased in Paris had five sheets of carbon paper. If he pressed the pen nib firmly enough on the top copy, he would make five more copies beneath to tear out and send off to family and supporters. He and Hélène had already decided to use the book as a joint journal, taking turns writing in it. They would also leave the top copy intact to keep a record of their correspondence.

The paddle wheels of the *Alémbé* beat the water in a steady rhythm as the boat chugged slowly upstream. It was the wet season, and a green wall of entwined vines wrapped around the towering trees lining the river.

"Never paddle too close to the river's edge," the captain, a Frenchman, told Albert when he saw him studying the shoreline. "There are plenty of snakes lying on tree branches that could drop into your boat. That's why we stay in the middle of the river. And we don't go any faster because of the many submerged trees and branches in this murky yellow water and the sandbars that shift with the strong currents." Albert nodded. This was a very different river from the Rhine, with its defined banks and rocky outcrops.

It didn't take Albert long to recognize two distinct tribes of Africans aboard the *Alémbé*. He was aware that Lambaréné was the boundary between the coastal Galoa people, who were tall, and the inland Fang or Pahouin people, who were much shorter. Some of the Galoa women had brightly patterned cloth draped around them, while the Pahouin women wore skirts made of woven grasses.

The riverboat steamed on hour after hour, stopping twice a day to take on wood for her boilers. The first stop was at a small village nestled by the river. The captain guided the boat into position in front of the village and dropped anchor. A plank was laid down from the shore to the vessel, and as the local African men began carrying logs aboard, Albert noticed the captain becoming agitated. Apparently the village men hadn't gathered as many logs as he needed. When all the logs were aboard the *Alémbé,* Albert watched as the captain counted out bottles of rum for payment.

A trader standing beside Albert explained, "There are no banks out here, no way to save money. The locals only need money to buy wives. They don't want more money, but they do want alcohol. It's the main form of payment for almost everything here in the jungle." Albert acknowledged the information with a nod. He remembered reading how French explorer Pierre de Brazza noted that alcohol use had decimated many villages in the Congo and Gabon areas. Albert realized this would be one of the many challenges he would deal with as a missionary doctor.

After three days the *Alémbé's* whistle blew, announcing to the traders at Lambaréné that they would be tying up at the landing there in half an hour. Albert watched as deckhands carried the luggage to the unloading bay, ready to be put ashore. The seventy crates and the piano were scheduled to arrive at Lambaréné when the paddle steamer made its return trip in two weeks. There wasn't enough cargo space for it on this trip.

Two canoes sped around a bend in the river and headed toward the boat. Each canoe had seven or eight boys standing upright, dipping long paddles furiously into the water. A white man sat in each canoe. The white man in the first canoe waved, and Albert waved back. He wondered if they were their welcoming committee.

The *Alémbé* stopped close to shore at Lambaréné, and a ramp was lifted into place. The Schweitzers' luggage was carried ashore. Albert and Hélène followed behind. No sooner had they stepped ashore than the two canoes pulled up at the landing spot. The two white men climbed out and introduced themselves. They were Noël Christol and René Ellenburger, two teachers from the Paris Evangelical Missionary Society school. Albert was delighted to meet them. Noël explained that the two canoes had raced each other for the honor of carrying the new missionaries to their post. Because Noël's canoe had won, the baggage was loaded into the second canoe while Albert and Hélène were helped into the other one.

The canoes were made from hollowed-out tree trunks with just a few inches between the waterline and the top of the canoe. Albert sat very still. He felt that one wrong move could easily capsize the vessel. Soon they were underway, the boys standing as they paddled and chanted. "Yah-nyeh, yah-nyeh, yah-nyeh—yneeeeeen-yak!" rang out across the water as the canoe glided out into the river. Albert gradually relaxed as he noted the effortless way the boys kept their balance and dipped their paddles in perfect time with each other. Although the mission station was named after the town of Lambaréné, which was located on the Big Island in the middle of the Ogowe River, the mission station was actually an hour's canoe journey down a tributary of the river.

The farther they paddled, the more amazed Albert was at the navigational skills of his escorts. Every turn in the river looked exactly like the last, with every creek passing through the same impenetrable tangle of trees and vines. At last, in the distance, Albert saw a cluster of buildings sitting on three small hills that rose from the river's edge, with a higher plateau behind and a larger hill rising above.

"That's known as American Hill," Noël said, pointing toward the large hill.

"Ah," Albert replied, thinking of all he'd read about the history of the mission. Thirty-seven years before, an American Presbyterian doctor and pastor named Robert Nassau was the first medical missionary to arrive at the location. "So that's where Dr. Nassau lived?" Albert inquired.

"Yes," Noël said. "The first house where he lived with his wife was farther down the hill, but after it was burned down three times by the native people, he and his wife retreated to the top of the hill, where they had a better view of what was going on around them. He was quite an amazing man. When he founded the mission here in 1874, the slave trade was illegal but still thriving in the interior jungle. The Fang and Galoa tribes were warring with each other to capture slaves, whom they ferried down to the coast to be sold. Dr. Nassau buried two wives and a son in the Congo, but he kept going for forty years before retiring."

"What an inspiration," Albert replied. "Before I left, the secretary of the Paris Evangelical Missionary Society gave me his address in the United States. I hope to write to him and let him know there is once again a doctor in Lambaréné. Which structure is the hospital?" he asked as they glided closer to the cluster of buildings.

"Actually, there isn't one," Noël replied. "I'm sorry to have to tell you this, but things haven't gone as planned. The timber price has skyrocketed lately, and all able-bodied African men are working for the timber merchants. Because we couldn't offer the same wages here at the mission, men left. We haven't even been able to get the roofing materials here. It's a shame, but this is how things are in Africa." He shrugged, then added, "Even when you think everything has been planned out, anything can go wrong."

"I see," Albert replied, struggling to digest the bad news. In two weeks, seventy crates of medical supplies were going to be delivered. Where would he put them all? More important, where would he treat his patients? The Paris Evangelical Missionary Society had promised him a house and a hospital, and he'd promised to do the rest. But how far would he get without the hospital?

The boys paddled closer to shore until they were close enough to jump out and drag the canoe onto the sandy beach. Eager hands reached out to steady Albert and Hélène as they stepped onto the shore. Bright-eyed children gathered around them, touching their clothes and staring up at them. One by one, three Europeans introduced themselves: Noël's wife, who ran the school; Hélène Humbert, her assistant; and Jacob Kast, a jack of all trades who taught in the boys' school.

The missionaries led Albert and Hélène up from the river's edge to their house. As they neared the place, Albert noticed that metal piles raised the structure twenty inches from the ground. The house itself was wooden and had a woven-tiled roof and a wide veranda that ran all the way around it.

A procession of children carried Albert and Hélène's belongings inside, after which Hélène Humbert escorted them all out again. Albert smiled at their curiosity. He could see that the children wanted to stay and watch everything being unpacked.

Twenty-one days had passed since Albert and Hélène had boarded the *Europe* at Pauillac in France, and suddenly here they were, in their own home at last. Albert was exhausted. He and Hélène sat down on wooden stools and enjoyed a few moments of silence. Then Albert hoisted a suitcase onto the bed and began to unpack.

Before long a bell rang, and the singsong voices of boys reciting something filled the air. Albert assumed it was nightly prayers, and he and Hélène followed the sound to where the schoolboys gathered with their teachers in front of their dormitory huts. As he listened, Albert was reminded of the primary classes at St. Nicholas Church in Strasbourg, where the children recited prayers aloud in German.

When the children had completed their prayers, Noël led the Schweitzers down the path to his house, where his wife had prepared dinner for them. Albert and Hélène enjoyed the food, though it was different from what they were used to. They ate fried bananas, which had a reddish tinge from being cooked in palm oil, and boiled fish and leaves that reminded Albert of bitter spinach.

After dinner, Mrs. Christol poured cups of hot coffee. "We have coffee bushes here," Noël told Albert, "and we drink a lot of coffee. It's better to have boiled drinks when you can. The water here can be dangerous." Albert nodded, recalling how he'd studied the huge problem of contaminated water during his tropical disease classes in Paris.

Later, Noël led Albert and Hélène back to their new home and waited until they had lit a kerosene lamp. Albert shut the door behind him and set about examining each window opening. The window frames had no glass in them but were covered by stretched mosquito netting. Albert knew that their entire medical mission rested on him and Hélène staying healthy, and one of their biggest challenges would be avoiding malaria. Thankfully, they knew how the disease was transmitted from one person to another. Two years before, Sir Ronald Ross had been knighted by the king of England for discovering that malaria was carried from person to person by mosquitos. Ross learned this in 1897 while working as an army surgeon in India. The latest textbooks Albert had used in medical school included diagrams of mosquito larvae and steps to prevent malaria from spreading. The two most important things were to sleep in a protected room under netting and to make sure there were no bodies of stagnant water—big or small—where mosquitos could breed near your dwelling or workplace.

Lying in bed that night, Albert listened to the strange sounds of the African jungle: cricket chirps, howling that he thought might be monkeys, and the distant beating of drums. He imagined that one day these would all sound as familiar to him as the rattling of trams in the streets of Strasbourg.

Drifting off to sleep, Albert was grateful to be exactly where he believed God wanted him to be.

Chapter 10

"Tonight, the Drums Will Beat for You"

The following morning René Ellenburger showed Albert around the mission property. "Is there anything we could use as a clinic until the hospital is built?" Albert asked as he looked around at the collection of thatch-roofed wooden buildings dotted across the three small hills.

René shook his head. "The school is full to overflowing. The house you moved into last night was the last empty space."

Albert wasn't sure what to say. Where would he put his supplies? And more important, where would he and Hélène treat patients?

As they continued to walk, Albert was surprised by the number of citrus trees flourishing on the property. He'd read that they were rare in this part of

Africa. A row of oil palms flanked the cleared area of the mission station, and behind them the jungle rose like a wall. "You'll see these wherever there's a settlement," René said, pointing up to the bunches of red fruit hanging between the leaves of the palm trees. "The locals crush them to get cooking oil. They say everything tastes better in palm oil," he added with a chuckle.

The entire mission station was about the size of eight soccer fields placed side by side. The house Albert and Hélène occupied was located toward the top of the center hill. On the hill to the right sat the boys' school buildings and the largest mission houses, and to the left were the girls' school and the remainder of the mission houses. As the men viewed the surroundings, René described how it was a constant struggle to hold back the jungle and stop it from reclaiming the mission compound.

Surveying the mission station, Albert noticed a small hut down the hill to the left of his house. It was a windowless structure, with a two-foot gap to let air flow through between the top of the walls and the roof. "What's that used for?" he asked, pointing to the hut.

"It was a henhouse, but no one uses it now. As you can see, it's falling down," René replied.

Albert walked over to the hut and pushed its door open. It creaked. Stepping inside, he looked up at the roof, which was made of woven squares of palm leaves. He noticed that the walls and floor were caked in chicken droppings. "Is this space available?" he asked.

"Of course, if you really want it," René responded.

"It's not ideal, but perhaps Hélène and I could do something with it, just to get us started," Albert said. "If we can scrub it clean enough, we could see one patient at a time here, though I don't see how we could store anything because of the gap at the top of the walls. We'll get some shelves built in our living room and make that into the pharmacy and storeroom."

"A good idea," René commented as he followed Albert out of the henhouse and closed and locked the door behind them. "You'll notice soon enough that everything here has to be kept under lock and key. My helpers tell me that's how the locals know that we value those things. If an item isn't locked up, they think we don't value it, and it has a habit of going missing."

Albert didn't say anything as he followed René toward the girls' school building. He noticed that René carried a ring of keys on his belt. This wasn't something he'd read about in articles in the mission magazine. It was odd to him to think of locking things up on a mission station, but apparently it was necessary to stop theft. But was that even the right word to use here? Did the Africans think taking something someone left unattended was stealing, or was it just the way things were out here in the jungle? Albert didn't know, but he had a feeling he was going to learn many lessons in patience as he adapted to life in a different culture.

During the walk around the mission property, René explained that the Africans used drums to relay information across vast swaths of jungle. "Tonight, the drums will beat for you," he informed Albert. "By morning everyone within two hundred miles of here will know Oganga has arrived in Lambaréné."

"Oganga?" Albert inquired.

"Yes," René nodded. "It means fetish man. It's the only word the Galoa have for a doctor. An oganga is the only man in their village they believe has the power to cause or cure pain and disease."

René also explained how most local people throughout the area were ruled by a belief in taboos—prohibited behaviors that would bring down the anger of the gods or cause a person to die. It was eye-opening for Albert to learn how these taboos dominated people's lives in the jungle. Group taboos applied to everyone, but each newborn was also given a personal taboo by a fetish man. These taboos could be anything from looking over a person's left shoulder to dancing in a circle or walking backward into the river, all of which could cause death. René explained how difficult it was to get local Christians to break their taboos, even if they believed that Jesus Christ had set them free.

"After the drums beat tonight, the desperate ones will come to you for help, though many of them will, I imagine, be beyond help."

Albert groaned inwardly when he heard René say this. His drugs and medical equipment were in crates that would not be delivered for another two weeks. He also had to ready the henhouse to serve as a clinic in which to treat patients.

That evening Albert and Hélène sat on their veranda, looking out at the light from the nearly full moon dancing on the surface of the river. Just as René had predicted, in the distance Albert could hear the beating of drums.

By the time he arose the next morning, Albert could hear many voices outside. As he stepped out onto the veranda, he was overwhelmed by the noise level. He was used to patients and their family members speaking privately to each other in quiet voices, but here in the jungle every detail appeared to be yelled at the top of a person's lungs. The people also spat freely and blew their noses through their fingers onto the ground. Albert shuddered as he thought of the germs being spread by this practice.

Walking among the crowd, Albert wished he had an interpreter so he could ask specific questions of people about their illnesses. Before leaving France he'd written to Noël asking him to hire a suitable person for the job. Noël had written back assuring Albert he'd found the perfect person to serve as his interpreter, a teacher named N'Zeng. But now N'Zeng was nowhere to be found, and René informed Albert that he was apparently stuck sixty miles away in his home village arguing over an inheritance. Albert prayed and trusted that something would work out, though he couldn't imagine what.

Despite the language barrier, as he walked among the people, Albert began to notice and identify several illnesses. Sleeping sickness slowed down a patient's speech and mental ability to the point where the person just wanted to sit staring into the distance or sleep for most of the day. And the afflicted person always walked with a shuffling gait. Left untreated, the disease was fatal. And then there was elephantiasis, where a part of the body, normally a leg or an arm, grew so large it became impossible for patients to drag themselves around. Albert learned from the doctor aboard the *Europe* that elephantiasis disfigured sufferers of the disease so much that many of them lost the will to live or were shunned from their homes and villages.

The stench of illness and decaying flesh filled the air as Albert continued inspecting the sick and assessing their conditions. Meanwhile flies and mosquitos buzzed around, carrying diseases from one person to another.

Soon René provided Albert with a bright student who spoke enough French to interpret a little of what the Africans wanted to say to Albert. Hélène brought out a small desk from the house, and Albert began his first clinic. He knew leprosy by the way it deadened the nerves in the skin. A person who didn't flinch when stuck by a pin was almost certainly suffering from the disease. People in the gathered group also suffered from other diseases such as swamp-fever, amoebic dysentery, and malaria, diseases Albert had only studied in textbooks until now. Others were suffering from hernias, ulcers, and abscesses. Albert could treat the simpler things with the few medicines he had brought in his personal luggage, but he had nothing to offer those with leprosy and some of the other diseases. And those suffering from hernias would have to wait, as there was not yet a clean, sterile place for Albert to perform surgeries.

The following day the crowd awaiting medical attention was bigger and continued to grow with each passing morning. To cope with the influx, Hélène set up a patient record-keeping system consisting of a long wooden box filled with index cards. On individual cards she wrote each patient's name and village along with a number that became the patient's permanent medical number. Then she recorded the reason for the visit and what treatment if any had been given. She also wrote the number on a cardboard disc with a string through it for the patient to hang around his or her neck until the next visit.

When they had any extra time, Albert and Hélène worked to fix up the henhouse as best they could. They chipped chicken droppings from the walls and floor, whitewashed the walls, and pushed the ends of palm fronds back through the woven tiles to patch the holes where the tiles had worn thin and allowed beams of blazing equatorial sunlight through.

At dusk, Albert and Hélène would sit on the veranda and look out across the river and surrounding jungle. One evening, Albert thought how the one thing he hadn't taken into account was the isolation of living on the edge of such an immense jungle. They were basically confined to the mission compound. Several trails led into the jungle from the mission station, but Albert had been warned not to venture down any of them without a good reason, a gun, and a native guide, especially at night. The jungle was inhabited by poisonous snakes and spiders along with dangerous animals, many of which hunted prey at night. Another terror was also lurking in the jungle of Gabon—Anyoto, or leopard men. Leopard men were members of a secret cult who wore leopard masks and draped themselves in leopard skins. They also attached razor-sharp metal claws to their hands and put metal-toothed mouthpieces in their mouths. The leopard men would stalk the jungle at night, tearing unsuspecting men and women to pieces with their claws and mouthpieces. The local people were terrified of them, believing they supernaturally transformed into actual leopards so they could kill. Albert didn't believe that part, but neither did he intend to wander off through the jungle bordering the mission property without a good reason.

Because the jungle was so dense, the area had no roads. The river was the only highway in and out of the mission station, and in its waters lurked other terrors, such as crocodiles and hippopotami. It was no place for a leisurely Sunday afternoon paddle.

As Albert thought about their location, his mind drifted back to his childhood in Gunsbach, where he used to wander for miles through the hills. He thought about Strasbourg, where he could freely bicycle around the cobblestoned city or head out into the countryside. But this place felt completely different. They were so isolated. The seven missionaries and the helpers they employed would be their constant and only companions for the next two years until they took a furlough. Albert wondered how different they would be when they returned home.

On the evening of April 26, 1913, Albert heard the far-off whistle of a steamer on the river. The next morning a paddler arrived to inform him that their crates and the piano had been unloaded at the Catholic mission station on the Big Island. Two missionaries and ten local men from N'Gomo soon arrived at Lambaréné and began ferrying the crates by canoe down to the Schweitzers' mission station. A local store owner at Lambaréné loaned Albert his enormous canoe to carry the piano downstream. It took three long days to deposit all the crates and the piano on the beach beside the river, then one by one the crates had to be carried up the hill to the Schweitzer home. Transporting the piano up the hill took a herculean effort by a number of men.

Once everything was moved from the beach, Albert looked around, feeling discouraged. Crates were piled on the veranda and in every room of the house, but there was nowhere to unpack them, nowhere to stow their contents. He thought of the hospital at Strasbourg with its neatly arranged rows of medicines and powders on the pharmacy shelves, the freshly sterilized sets of surgical instruments laid out precisely on clean white towels in the operating room. That all seemed a million miles away from the jungle of Gabon. Albert glumly asked himself if it was possible to reach even half that degree of cleanliness and order out here.

Chapter 11

Outpost of the Kingdom of God

The next morning Albert talked to Jacob Kast, the mission's handyman, about building shelves along the walls of their living room. Jacob took some measurements and made a sketch in a notebook. "I think I can build something like this using the wood from the packing crates," he said.

Albert looked at the sketch and said, "This design will do perfectly."

Albert and Hélène unpacked one box at a time. Then Jacob pried the nails out of each box, sawed the sides in half, and turned the wood into shelves. When each set of shelves was complete, Albert and Hélène arranged their medical supplies on them while Jacob constructed the next set. It took a day and a half to unpack all the crates and organize their contents on the new shelves lining the living room.

Albert was pleased with the result. Things might not be as well organized as at the hospital in Strasbourg, but the shelves did the job. Now it was time to get the old henhouse ready for patients. Jacob used scraps of wood and attached them to the henhouse walls to make more shelves, and René gave Albert a camp bed to use as an examination table. There was no room for anything else.

Each morning people gathered outside the new clinic to see Albert. Sometimes he was relieved when he had to leave the clinic to walk up to his house to get drugs for a patient. So many of the men, women, and children he was treating suffered from the most painful medical conditions he could imagine. Getting drugs for them gave him a moment to compose himself. Soon after Albert arrived at Lambaréné, an old African man told him, "Among us everyone is ill. Our country devours her own children." Surrounded by so much suffering, Albert found himself agreeing with the old man's assessment. Nothing, he decided, could have adequately prepared a European doctor for the medical conditions here.

Still, Albert thrived on challenges. He wrote a letter to his sister outlining the medical situations he saw and ended it with, "Evenings I go to bed dead-tired, but in my heart I am profoundly happy that I am serving at the outpost of the kingdom of God!"

Albert was also grateful for Hélène and the fact that she'd trained as a nurse. She took responsibility for washing and rewinding bandages, sterilizing medical instruments, and keeping patient records in order.

Albert decided not to do surgeries until the new hospital was built. It seemed safer to wait until he had a fully enclosed and sterile operating room. But that changed one morning when a man who was doubled over in pain was led into the clinic. Albert examined him and determined the man was suffering from a strangulated hernia, a condition in which an internal organ pushes through an opening in the muscle tissue that should have held it in place. By now Albert had noted that hernias were more prevalent around Lambaréné than in Alsace. Once he had the new operating room, he expected to do a lot of hernia surgeries. But a strangulated hernia needed immediate attention, or this man would die. Even if it had to be done in a henhouse, Albert knew he must perform emergency surgery.

Albert sent Hélène to ask Noël if he had any better ideas. Soon a plan was made. Noël gave the boys the afternoon off school and then wiped down the desks and other surfaces in the empty classroom with disinfectant. Meanwhile Hélène collected the needed towels, sheets, and bandages and prepared the anesthetic. Albert set about sterilizing the surgical instruments and arranged them in the schoolroom for the operation.

That afternoon Albert and Hélène worked as a surgical team for the first time. Albert wielded the scalpel while Hélène administered the anesthetic and monitored the patient's vital signs. Much to Albert's relief, the surgery went well, with no complications.

Once word was out that Albert could operate on hernias, he knew that many more people would find their way to his doorstep. But because of the labor shortage, there was still no new hospital in sight. René assured Albert that since the rainy season was now ending, the men would return to their villages, and some might be willing to build the hospital. It was frustrating for Albert to wait, but he had no other option.

Not long after the emergency hernia surgery, a young man from the Galoa tribe came to receive a checkup. His name was Joseph Azoawani. As Joseph sat on the edge of the camp bed, he entered into lively conversation in French with Albert. Joseph's French was excellent, and he explained to Albert that he'd worked for a white man who taught him to speak fluently. He also said he could speak nine regional dialects, including Pahouin and his Galoa mother tongue. Suddenly Albert realized he had the perfect interpreter sitting right in front of him. Albert offered him a job, and Joseph accepted on the spot. It didn't take long for Albert to appreciate what a gift Joseph was. It was such a relief to be able to communicate thoroughly with the patients through a skilled interpreter.

Joseph did have one quirk Albert found amusing. Joseph had learned anatomy from cooking meat for his previous employer, and he continued referring to human body parts that way. "This patient has a sore left cutlet," he would tell Albert, or "an infection in his lower right brisket." Albert tried correcting Joseph, but Joseph was stubborn, and in the end Albert accepted Joseph's unique contributions to medical conversations.

Although he'd never been taught to read or write, Joseph was unusually observant. Within a week he had learned to identify the various bottles of pills and medicines by the shapes of the words printed on their labels. Albert watched many times to make sure that Joseph selected the correct medicines, and he never saw Joseph make a single mistake. Before long he trusted him implicitly.

Now that he had a language assistant, Albert was able to bring order to the unruly patients and their families who showed up each morning. He asked himself what the most important things were that he wanted to tell them. As they came to mind, he wrote them down. "1) Spitting near the doctor's house is strictly forbidden." Spitting was a big problem, especially since diseases were transmitted through contact with bodily fluids. Each time Albert saw or heard someone spit, he could feel his blood pressure rise. He knew he would probably never stop the locals from spitting altogether, but at least he could ban it near his house and the clinic where so many sick people sat or stood close together.

Albert continued writing. "2) Those who are waiting must not yell." Again, this was something that grated on his nerves. Sometimes it was so noisy outside the clinic it was impossible to call the next patient.

"3) Patients and their friends must each bring enough food for one day." Food was a problem. Sometimes patients had to wait all day to be seen, and as they waited, they got hungry. Albert didn't want patients and their family members arriving at the clinic and expecting the mission to take care of all their needs, including food, for as long as they stayed. He firmly believed that patients should help in their own care as best they could. That included bringing enough food with them to eat for a day.

"4) Anyone who spends a night on mission property without the doctor's permission will be sent away without any medicine." Albert knew this sounded harsh, but the patients and their families sometimes invaded the school dormitories, demanding that students vacate their beds so the adults could sleep in them. Not only was it disruptive to the school, but it also ran the risk of infecting schoolchildren with many illnesses.

"5) All bottles and tin cans in which medicines are given must be returned." Albert doubted he would get 100 percent compliance, since anything made of glass or tin was precious in the humid jungle. He suspected people sometimes visited the clinic just so they could receive a pill bottle or tin. They prized them as fetishes, hanging them around their necks to ward off evil spirits.

"6) In the middle of the month, when the steamer has gone upriver, only urgent cases can be brought to the doctor. When the steamer comes from the coast, all others may come, as the steamer will be bringing more medicines for the doctor to give out."

Albert asked Joseph to memorize the six rules and announce them each morning in French, Pahouin, Galoa, and the other dialects he spoke, to those gathered outside the clinic.

Slowly Joseph started taking over some of Hélène's workload. Albert observed that most of his patients and their families were deathly afraid of touching blood or pus. Joseph, however, was not, and he cheerfully washed bandages and held bloated limbs steady while Albert lanced boils or cleaned out abscesses.

The local Africans blamed many kinds of sickness on "the worm." To them the worm entered their bodies through the feet, and if they were lucky, it exited through the top of the head. Albert basically agreed with their view. Worms and parasites entering their bodies were the root cause of most deadly tropical diseases. In order to diagnose a patient's health problem, Albert often spent hours hunched over a microscope, examining blood samples for various parasites.

By mid-June 1913, Albert felt he had a clearer picture of what medicines he needed for the next few months. He wrote to friends and supporters in Strasbourg to explain the situation:

> I am now in a position to judge which medications are the most important. They are quinine; sodium sulfur; chaulmoogra oil, which is

> effective when blended with olive oil (to treat leprosy); sulfur (for scabies); potassium iodide (for a number of skin diseases); all cardiotonics (since the number of people suffering from heart disease and pneumonia is shockingly high); anything required for the preparation of soothing and desiccant ointments; bromine (epilepsy) and arsenicals. . . .
>
> As long as the medical barracks are incomplete, working here is an arduous task. I spend my days in an old chicken coop without windows. . . . The people are very grateful for what we do for them. The misery is enormous.

In follow-up letters Albert appealed to his friends to send old clothing to a small band of church women at St. Nicholas Church in Strasbourg. The women would cut the items of clothing into strips for bandages and send them to Lambaréné. Most of all, Albert begged people to save glass bottles and tins for use in the clinic.

Albert and Hélène celebrated their first wedding anniversary on June 18, 1913. They went for a walk on the sandbar, which the low dry-season river level had exposed. They had to tread carefully, as this was the time of year that crocodiles became restless and were more likely to attack.

In late July, laborers were hired to start laying the foundation for the first hospital building. The structure would consist of four rooms—two large rooms for consulting and surgeries, and two smaller rooms to serve as a dispensary and a sterilizing room. Once the workers had poured the foundation and the cement floors, they began erecting framework. The work went slowly. To Albert it seemed that every time he turned his back the laborers stopped working to smoke cigarettes and argue about things going on in their villages. Yet they still expected to be paid for a full day's work. Albert grew so frustrated he talked to Joseph about it.

"Don't be so anxious, Oganga. After all, it is your own fault," Joseph told him. "The men have come to work for you. When you're not there, they do not work. Why would they? If you want them to work, you must stay and work beside them."

To Albert's German way of thinking, this was a ridiculous way to look at things. But he knew he wasn't in Europe anymore and had to accept the reality of the situation. He began setting aside several hours each day to dig and hammer alongside the local men. To his surprise, the pace of work sped up.

In early November the new hospital building, with its corrugated iron roof and sides, was ready to open. Medical equipment and supplies were moved in. Flower garlands festooned the doors as the building was dedicated to the work of God in Gabon. No sooner was the opening ceremony over than Albert broke ground on the next two buildings—a waiting room for patients and a sixteen-bed ward. These buildings would use woven raffia panels to cover the roof and sides. And now that Albert understood how to keep the locals working, things moved along at a steady pace.

By December the waiting room and ward were complete. The only problem was a lack of beds in the new ward. To rectify this, Albert decided it was time for the friends and relatives of the patients to help out. He grabbed a stick and etched sixteen rectangles into the dirt floor where he wanted the beds to go. Then he told family members that their sick relatives would not sleep on a bed unless they built it for them. Before long the interior of the ward was a hive of activity. Women twisted creepers into ropes to lash the beds together while men shaped logs they'd cut into bedposts, rails, and slats. Once a bed was lashed together, dried grass was piled on the slats to form a mattress. When the sixteen beds were finished, patients were escorted from their makeshift quarters in the boat shed to the new ward.

Christmas was a joyful time at Lambaréné. The missionaries gave each other homemade gifts, and Albert played carols on his piano Christmas Eve. On Christmas Day they ate together as one big community and shared various traditional nuts and dried fruits family members had sent from home.

On New Year's Day Albert and Hélène talked about looking forward to a fruitful year ahead. They had their new hospital, and Albert set his sights on the next building—a separate ward for patients suffering from sleeping sickness.

The first six months of 1914 rolled by smoothly, with Albert and Hélène keeping busy managing the hospital and tending patients. In the evenings they climbed the hill to their home, tired yet fulfilled. To relax, Albert enjoyed playing Bach on his piano late into the evening.

Each arrival of a riverboat at Lambaréné brought letters and packages for the Schweitzers. Albert and Hélène read the letters and talked about them, and Albert would pore over the newspaper clippings his father sent. The more he read, the more concerned he became about the political situation in Europe. In mid-July Albert's father sent a series of clippings describing how on June 28, 1914, Archduke Franz Ferdinand, heir to the throne of the Austro-Hungarian Empire, had been assassinated in Sarajevo, the Bosnian capital, by a young Serbian nationalist. The clippings that arrived on the next riverboat described how the killing of the archduke had set in motion a series of events in Europe. Kaiser Wilhelm II had promised Germany's support to the Austro-Hungarians as they retaliated against Serbia, whom they blamed for the assassination.

On August 5, at the height of the dry season, Albert sent Joseph to the Big Island post office to mail some medicine to a Cape Lopez missionary. Joseph returned with terrible news. "There's no mail coming or going on the river. The postmaster says you are at war; the Germans are fighting the French and the British, and all steamboats in Gabon have been requisitioned by the military."

Albert sat down to take in the news. He'd been half expecting that something like this would happen following the archduke's assassination, though he'd hoped intelligent people would be able to work out their differences without resorting to war. He had been too optimistic. He would have time to think about that later, but at the moment, Albert knew he had to consider his and Hélène's safety. They were German citizens serving in a French colony and were now perceived as enemies. Somehow they needed to escape north to German-controlled Cameroon. Albert rushed to find Hélène. The two talked about the situation as they packed a few belongings and made preparations to leave the following morning, though Albert had no idea how they would make it through the dense jungle to Cameroon.

At twilight that evening, as Albert and Hélène tried to formalize their escape plan, a dozen armed African men dressed in the uniforms of the French Colonial Forces pulled their canoe onto the beach at the mission station. From the veranda Albert watched them march up the hill to his house. He recognized one of the soldiers, a man he'd treated for an infected gash on his shoulder.

"Get inside your house and don't come out," the group leader shouted, pointing his rifle at Albert. "You are ordered not to speak to anyone. You are under arrest in the name of the French government."

Albert and Hélène did as they were told. The world, it seemed to Albert, even this tiny outpost in Gabon, had gone mad.

Chapter 12

Reverence for Life

It seemed senseless to Albert that he and Hélène were considered to be enemy aliens when clearly they were in French Equatorial Africa to bring medical aid to the native population. How could someone order all medical work stopped because of something happening so far away? But that was exactly what had happened, and Albert realized he needed to look at this confinement as an opportunity. According to their chief guard, they could do whatever they liked, as long as they didn't talk to anyone else or leave the house. Possibilities ran through Albert's mind. He'd recently started setting aside time in the evenings to work on a new book he planned to write on the history of civilization and what it means. It was a topic he'd been pondering since university. And there was a piece of Bach's music he wanted to perfect on the piano. Now, in an unexpected way, he had time for both.

The soldiers guarding them started off being strict, but within a week Albert and Hélène were permitted to talk with the French missionaries who brought them food. The guards even allowed them to post letters once they had checked them. This was a welcome concession: mail was the lifeblood of Albert and Hélène's communication with their family and friends. Albert wrote a barrage of letters to people he knew in France with any kind of influence. They included Charles Widor, members of the Bach Society of Paris, even his Uncle Auguste. He begged them to pressure the French government to allow him to continue his medical work.

Albert and Hélène's days settled into routine. Albert played the piano, read, prayed, wrote, and looked out over the languid river as it flowed by the mission station. Hélène did much the same. Yet they could not escape the sadness of being unable to offer help to the many people who clearly needed it. It seemed such a waste.

A month later, a messenger with a note from the district commandant's office visited Albert. The message he carried made no sense. It merely repeated old information about his alien status—things Albert already knew. More confusing, the messenger looked too sickly to be carrying a message to a missionary outpost. What was going on? Then Albert understood. It wasn't the message but the messenger he was supposed to pay attention to. Despite Albert's being officially barred from practicing medicine and running the hospital, the commandant wanted him to treat the sick messenger. Albert happily did so. Afterward the commandant sent several more messages, each delivered by a sick man, whom Albert treated.

During November, a messenger from the resident general of Gabon arrived. The message he carried stated that Albert and Hélène, who had been under house arrest for four long months, were now permitted to continue their medical work at Lambaréné.

Christmas 1914 came and went, followed by Albert's fortieth birthday on January 14, 1915. But there wasn't much to celebrate. Albert could barely imagine what his family was going through back home in Alsace and France. Four years before Albert's birth, when Alsace became part of Germany, those living there were given the choice of staying and becoming German citizens or leaving to live in France. Albert's two uncles, Charles and Auguste Schweitzer, chose to leave and moved to Paris, while his father stayed in Alsace. As a result, members of the Schweitzer family were now on opposite sides of the war.

At the start of the war, many Frenchmen living in French Equatorial Africa were ordered back to France to join the army. Slowly, word of the fate of these men trickled back to Africa. By February 1915 ten of the men who had been called up from Gabon had been killed in the fighting. When the local Africans heard of the deaths, they were incredulous. One local chief asked Albert what was going on. "You white men preach about love and hope, but you are killing each other. I have come to ask you why. How many people have been killed in this war of yours? Ten?"

"More than ten," Albert replied.

"Don't you have to pay for each dead man? How can anyone afford that much? Why don't you have a long talk and end this killing?"

Albert was taken aback. He had three doctoral degrees from one of the top universities in Europe, and this chief who had never been to school or traveled beyond his jungle home had asked him a question he could not answer. All Albert could do was admit that he had been asking himself the same question.

"And do the white men eat each other at such times?" the chief inquired.

"No," Albert said. "They leave the bodies where they fall."

The chief sniffed. "Then there's nothing to be gained. It is cruel to kill for no reason."

Albert could only nod. The war taking place in Europe indeed seemed senseless.

As 1915 progressed, the situation in the Ogowe River Basin grew worse. Before the war, over 150,000 tons of hardwood trees had been felled in the area, with their trunks floated downriver to be loaded onto ships at Cape Lopez. Since timber workers were paid twice as much as other workers, that was how most men were employed. The job gave them enough money to buy enamel basins instead of using traditional wooden bowls. They could also purchase imported rice from their employers, since they didn't have time to plant their traditional manioc crops or clear new land for banana trees. But with all available ships requisitioned and the North Atlantic Ocean part of a war zone, timber could no longer be exported. As a result, the jobs paying high wages evaporated, while adequate crops hadn't been planted in years. Famine began to stalk the people in the river basin.

Albert realized that much of what was happening in Gabon, as in many other parts of Africa, was due to the European scramble to divide and colonize African territories. The Europeans wanted to exploit the land for raw materials, ignoring the good of the African people. Now the war was pitting the world's two largest colonial empires—Great Britain and France—against the third largest, Germany. This meant that their African colonies were automatically being drawn into the war as well. It seemed nonsensical to Albert that Melanesians in New Guinea were fighting Australians in the name of Germany, and hundreds of thousands of Indian men from the India Expeditionary Force fought alongside their British colonial overlords against the Ottoman Empire.

Albert and Hélène did what they could to help the local people, but their supplies were dwindling fast. Albert had brought a stash of gold coins with him from Europe for emergencies, but now he was down to his last few. By August 1915 they had no medicines, no kerosene, and no hope of seeing more anytime soon, since most of his supplies, which came from German Alsace, were no longer allowed into Gabon. Albert had no choice but to inform Joseph that his wages would need to be halved. Joseph responded that his dignity wouldn't allow him to work for so little. He packed his belongings and left the hospital. It was a bitter blow for Albert and Hélène, who had come to rely on Joseph's help with so many things.

Without reliable help or supplies, the work of the hospital ground to a near standstill. Once more Albert found himself with time to ponder his book about civilization. Since starting the writing process, he'd struggled with how to describe what he believed: that all life is special; that people shouldn't kill each other, or even animals, merely because they could; and that if you remove one group of animals or plants, you upset the balance of nature in a fundamental way.

During September 1915, Albert needed to travel to treat a sick missionary. He rode in one of two canoes pulled by a small towboat. It turned out to be a slow trip. The towboat had barely enough power to move itself and the two canoes forward against the current. As they chugged along, Albert used the time to work on his book. He scribbled pages of notes—anything he could think of—with a pencil as he tried to get to the heart of what he wanted to say. Late in the afternoon, as the sun cast long orange rays across the river, and the towboat carefully made its way past a group of hippopotami, a phrase came to Albert's mind: "Reverence for Life." Instantly he knew that this was the missing piece. If human civilization was to make real progress, then it must embrace the idea that all life was created by God and is sacred in its own way. Humans must approach nature as a beautiful gift that should not be squandered.

Albert remembered back to over thirty years before. He'd been a young schoolboy looking for acceptance when he agreed to go bird hunting with Heinrich Brasch in the hills above Gunsbach. He thought about how, as they closed in on a flock of stonechats resting in a beech tree, he had been overcome with dread at what they were about to do—kill innocent birds with slingshots. In the end Albert had thrown down his slingshot and run toward the beech tree, scaring the birds away before Heinrich could take a shot. He'd always been proud of his decision to protect the stonechats, and now he had a deeper understanding of why he had done what he did. His action had been motivated by a deep reverence for life. God had made and given those stonechats life, and because of that, they were sacred.

The revelation gave Albert the necessary drive to continue writing, though at times he was slowed down by bouts of anemia and bleeding sores on his feet.

As the war dragged on, many Europeans throughout the area came to stay at the hospital. Albert didn't have drugs to treat most of them, but he knew that many were coming for companionship as much as anything else. Upon arriving in Africa, nearly all Europeans were advised to return home once every two years to build up their health. But like the Schweitzers, the war was forcing Europeans to stay much longer than intended. As a result, they were in desperate need of a nutritional boost, a good dentist, and a long rest. Albert could offer them only the last of these. He and Hélène often moved out of their bedroom to sleep on the veranda in order to give their guests a solid bed and some privacy in the hope that it would rejuvenate them and restore them to good health.

Meanwhile, mail from Europe was sporadic. Everyone exchanged any news they received in their letters, but most of it was from a French perspective. It felt strange to Albert to hear of "victories" in France that from the German perspective were "defeats." News from the Western Front was particularly disturbing. This front marked the edge of the fighting between Germany and Allied forces, including France and Great Britain. It ran from the Belgian coast through eastern France, all the way to the border with Switzerland. Part of the front ran through western Alsace, and Albert could only imagine the damage being done there to his beautiful homeland.

In mid-August 1916, Albert received news from Gunsbach informing him that his mother had been killed. On July 3 she and Albert's father were out walking in the countryside when an out-of-control horse, ridden by a German cavalryman, galloped around a corner and trampled her. She sustained serious injuries, and despite receiving immediate medical care, she died the following day. Albert wished he could be with his father and the rest of the family at that moment, but he was thousands of miles away.

By October 1916, Albert and Hélène agreed they needed a long break. They were both weak, and their health had been worn down. By now work at the hospital was at a complete stop. They had no food to give patients, no medicines to treat them with, and no staff to help. And they had no hope of more drugs or money being allowed into French Equatorial Africa from Germany. Albert and Hélène shuttered their house at Lambaréné and headed for Cape Lopez. There the Paris Evangelical Missionary Society loaned them money to rent a house by the river estuary on the condition that they also use it as a guest house for other exhausted missionaries. Soon another missionary couple from Alsace, Leon and Georgette Morel, joined them at the house. Finally, Albert let himself relax. He swam in the ocean, caught fish, took walks with Hélène, read books, and wrote. It was just what he needed, except for receiving the relentless updates about the carnage in Europe.

During the second week of April 1917, more than two and a half years after the start of the war, news reached Cape Lopez that on April 6 the United States had joined the French and British to fight the Germans. Albert hoped the move would end the fighting sooner rather than later.

After staying at the coast much longer than anticipated and feeling rested and rejuvenated, Albert and Hélène returned to Lambaréné in August 1917. It felt good to be back again. Albert felt strong enough to think about reopening the hospital as an outpatient clinic if he could get supplies. However, before he could do so, his and Hélène's fortunes changed yet again. This time it came in the form of an official order from Brazzaville, the main administrative center for French Equatorial Africa. The newly formed French government of Georges Clemenceau had ordered that all enemy aliens in French Equatorial Africa be transferred to France immediately. Albert and Hélène were given twenty-four hours to pack one fifty-five-pound bag each and prepare to leave. It was agonizing for Albert as he went over what to do with his precious new book manuscript. He'd written it in German and realized any French official who laid eyes on it would probably confiscate the manuscript on the spot. What should he do with it? He decided to leave it with one of the other missionaries at Lambaréné, instructing him to hold on to it until the war was over and Albert could send for it. As a precaution he copied the headings and notes on the key points of the book into French to take with him.

Albert and Hélène were escorted back downriver to Cape Lopez, where they wearily climbed the gangway to board the steamship *Afrique*, bound for Bordeaux, France. A steward guided them to their cabin. A French colonial officer stopped by to tell them that throughout the voyage they could not leave their cabin or talk to anyone except the steward, and that once a day they would be taken on an escorted walk around the ship for exercise. Albert hardly cared. He was so exhausted from packing up and contemplating what might happen to his manuscript that he looked forward to sitting in solitude.

The steward did everything possible to make Albert and Hélène comfortable. He confessed he was doing so because one of Albert's previous patients, a timber company owner from upriver, had voyaged on the *Afrique* several months before. He had told the steward about Albert's medical work and asked him to treat the doctor from Lambaréné with care and respect if Albert was ever a passenger or a prisoner aboard the ship. Albert was cheered to hear this, but there was no hiding the fact that he and Hélène were returning to France as prisoners of war.

As he sat in the cabin day after day, Albert couldn't help but think of the voyage to Africa four and a half years earlier. He'd left France with the best wishes and prayers of the French people. He had been sent out from the Paris Evangelical Missionary Society, and he even had with him a specially made piano—a gift from the Bach Society of Paris. He was returning to the same place from which he had left, except now he was a prisoner of war being transported to an unknown future in a war-ravaged enemy country.

Chapter 13

Enemy Aliens

Icy rain fell as the wrought-iron gate slammed behind Albert and Hélène. They had walked the two miles south from the Port of the Moon in the heart of Bordeaux to a two-story white stone building on a narrow road. He prayed they would get the chance to rest and recover, as well as receive some warm clothing, now that they'd arrived at their destination.

However, inside the building things went from bad to worse. They were housed in a drafty room with bare stone walls and floors and no heating. It was cold by any standard, but for Albert and Hélène, who were still accustomed to living just below the equator, it was freezing. In the cold conditions, Hélène's cough grew worse, and Albert could see that she was exhibiting the telltale symptoms of tuberculosis.

Then they both became ill with dysentery—something, ironically, Albert had avoided during his four and a half years living in Africa.

A guard told Albert they were housed in a temporary prison and would soon be transferred elsewhere. Albert wondered if he and Hélène would be separated, sent deeper into France, or shipped on to the rumored holding camp for enemy aliens in Egypt. He didn't know; he just prayed that he and Hélène stayed together.

Just before Christmas 1917, after three weeks in Bordeaux, Albert and Hélène were loaded onto a train headed south. Along the way, other German-speaking prisoners were put aboard the train. Although Albert didn't know their exact destination, he knew they were headed toward the Pyrenees Mountains that separate France and Spain. After Albert and Hélène had been sitting on a freezing wooden bench in a drafty carriage for seven hours, the train hissed to a halt, and everyone was ordered off. Albert and Hélène had arrived at Garaison, where they were transferred to a chapel and old monastery built in 1540 to honor the Virgin Mary's healing powers.

Albert had often dreamed of spending Christmas in France, but this was not what he had imagined. As they were led through the monastery gates, he noticed diversity among the people being held there. At Garaison Albert discovered that he was one of about seventeen hundred civilians caught up on the wrong side of the war for various reasons. It didn't take him long to learn the stories of some of his fellow internees: painters from Paris; Austrian and German dressmakers and shoemakers who worked for large Parisian companies; bank directors, engineers, architects, and businessmen who'd been living in French colonies. There were Catholic missionary priests from the Sahara, wearing white robes and red fezzes; travelers from North America, South America, China, and India who'd been captured at sea; and crews of captured German and Austrian merchant ships. There were also prisoners from elsewhere, including Turks, Arabs, and Greeks.

The day after arriving at Garaison, Albert was shivering in the courtyard when an internee walked up and introduced himself as Gerhard Borkeloh. "We don't know each other," he told Albert, "but I must thank you. You saved my wife's life."

"How so?" Albert asked.

"Do you remember Richard Classen, who worked for a Hamburg timber company?"

Albert nodded. He did remember the man. Richard had been a patient at the hospital in Lambaréné until the French arrested him and sent him off somewhere as a prisoner of war. Before Richard was taken away, the French colonial soldiers had allowed Albert to supply him with a collection of medicines. Before packing the medicines in Richard's knapsack, Albert had labeled each medicine with specific instructions on its use and dosage.

"Richard ended up in the same camp in eastern France as my wife and I. She was in a bad way, and we were able to treat her with the drugs from

Lambaréné. Without your help, I don't think she would have survived this long," Gerhard said.

Albert clapped him on the shoulder. "I'm glad to hear the medicines weren't confiscated, and that they reached people to whom they were useful."

Gerhard nodded. "I will forever be in your debt. Is there anything you want here? I'm a carpenter. I could make you something."

Albert smiled. "I do need something. If you can find wood, I would love a desk for my room so I can write and practice organ finger work on it."

Two days later Gerhard knocked on Albert's door. He carried a wooden desk made from boards torn loose from the attic wall. Albert was grateful for the gesture, and he and Hélène put the desk to good use.

When Albert inquired about medical opportunities to serve his fellow internees, he was informed that he was the only doctor among them, but that his services were not needed. An elderly doctor who lived in town visited the camp when necessary. Albert was shocked. All around people were sick with malaria, dysentery, and various worm infections. How could a local doctor in the Pyrenees know the treatment for such tropical diseases? Albert asked to see the internment camp governor and volunteered his tropical medicine expertise. The governor turned him down.

Meanwhile, Albert was becoming a popular figure around the prison. When the members of a gypsy band captured while playing at a Paris nightclub recognized him as a well-known organist, they invited Albert to their private music practices. And after roll call in the courtyard twice a day, many of the internees stood talking and exchanging with Albert any news or rumors they'd heard. Other internees formed small groups at which they gave talks on anything they were knowledgeable about. Albert greatly appreciated this because it helped fill the time. He learned many interesting things about finance, architecture, growing grain, factory construction, equipment, and furnace building. *Maybe one day,* he told himself, *I will be able to use this knowledge at Lambaréné.*

Thankfully, Hélène's parents found a way to mail them small amounts of money along with some woolen fabric. A dressmaker among the internees volunteered to make Hélène a suit, for which Hélène was most grateful. The monastery's stone walls made Christmas 1917 the coldest and bleakest that Albert and Hélène had ever experienced.

Hélène turned thirty-nine on January 25, 1918, and the gypsy band serenaded the event outside her bedroom window. It was a high point in their dismal existence.

Two months later, on March 27, Albert and Hélène were ordered to pack their belongings and prepare to move. They soon found themselves seated in a double-decker train carriage heading east. When the train stopped at the Saint-Rémy-de-Provence station, Albert and Hélène were escorted off and taken by horse-drawn wagon up to another old former monastery, the Monastery of Saint Paul-de-Mausole. Like Garaison, this monastery served as an internment camp, one of seventy the French government had set up for enemy aliens. However, this place was much smaller than Garaison, with only 105 imprisoned there, all from Alsace. As Albert walked through the gates, many of the internees lined up to greet him. For the first time in years, he saw familiar faces from his past. There was Jean Iltis, a schoolmaster from Gunsbach, and Peter Liebrich, one of his former seminary students at the Theological College of St. Thomas, who was now the unofficial camp pastor. Although Albert had enjoyed the diverse group of people at Garaison, he felt a certain relief in being among people he'd grown up around. They all spoke the same Alsatian low-German dialect and knew people and places in common. Some of them knew Albert's brother-in-law, Jules Ehrtsmann, in Colmar, or had visited Gunsbach and heard his father preach.

Soon after arriving at the Monastery of Saint Paul-de-Mausole, Albert had a vague sense he'd been there before. He noticed something familiar about the long room in which they stayed during the day, with its overhead pipes and single cast-iron stove at one end. Not only that—he was sure he recognized the view from the second-story window. In time, he learned the reason. Albert *had* seen it all before—in the sketches and paintings done by Vincent van Gogh, who'd been confined thirty years before.

On Good Friday, Peter Liebrich asked Albert to preach at the church service. It was a moving moment for Albert as he looked out over the gathered internees, each with a personal story of how he or she got there. But who knew how their stories would end? The war seemed to be far from over.

After the service, one of the guards announced some war news. The Germans had fired a long-range gun at Paris, and its shell had landed on Saint-Gervais Church during their morning service. The church roof had collapsed, and over eighty worshipers were presumed dead. Upon hearing the news, Albert asked Hélène to allow him time alone. He went to their room, closed the door, sat on the bed, and wept. Albert wept for all those who'd been killed in Paris, he wept for the beautiful church of Saint-Gervais, but most of all he wept for the complete, senseless misery the war was causing so many people on both sides. *What,* he wondered, *will the world be like when this war ends and people assess the horror they have wrought on each other?*

The internees at the monastery had a surprising amount of freedom. The internment camp governor was a retired police commissioner from Marseilles and wasn't interested in punishing his prisoners. Instead, he tried to make their lives easier in any way he could. Whenever a delegation went to him and asked if something was permitted, he responded with a smile. "Nothing is permitted! But there are certain things that are tolerated, if you show yourselves reasonable!"

From the start, Albert liked the governor, who had guards escort those who were strong enough on a walk into the village twice a week. Sadly, as they walked, the internees were met with taunts from the local people. But neither Albert nor Hélène was well enough to keep up with the pace of this long walk. Thankfully, the camp governor himself took them and the other weaker prisoners for shorter walks.

By now France had been at war for three and a half years and French doctors were in short supply, since many of them had been killed at the battlefront. As a result, Saint-Rémy was soon without a doctor. The camp governor asked Albert, despite his suffering from dysentery, to take over the position. Albert agreed, and before long people from the village were begging him for treatment. Albert was allowed to leave the monastery under escort to do so.

Although the mail coming in and out of the internment camp was censored, bit by bit Albert pieced together what was happening in the war. The Bolshevik Revolution and resulting civil war in Russia had led to a cessation of fighting on the Eastern Front. No longer fighting the Russians, Germany quickly moved its troops to reinforce the Western Front, especially now that the United States had entered the war on the side of France, Great Britain, and the Allies. Already fresh American troops were streaming into France. Nonetheless, Germany was making a determined effort to push farther into France. Albert hoped it would all be over soon. He wondered how many more people would have to die before reason prevailed.

In March, around the time that Albert and Hélène had arrived, prisoners began leaving the monastery. Germany and France had reached an agreement that allowed an exchange of prisoners. At first nonmilitary prisoners over forty-eight years of age who'd been in captivity for more than eighteen months were exchanged. Albert hoped it was only a matter of time before he and Hélène were released. It took another three and a half months, but at midnight on July 12, 1918, Albert and Hélène were awakened and told to prepare to leave. Albert was relieved. At thirty-nine years of age, Hélène had recently realized she was pregnant and expecting a baby in January. Albert was concerned about her health and hoped to be able to provide more nutritious food once they were released.

At sunrise, Albert and Hélène carried their belongings to the internment camp courtyard for inspection. From the internment camp, they were transported to the railway station and put on a train headed north to Lyon and then northeast toward Switzerland. Albert was glad to be allowed to take the notes on his civilization book that he'd been writing at both Garaison and Saint-Rémy.

The train grew longer as carriages carrying prisoners from other internment camps were hitched to it. When they reached the Swiss border, the internees had to wait for hours. Albert stared out the window, hoping that everything was going to be all right. At last a telegram arrived, saying that the German train carrying French and Allied prisoners had arrived at Constance, a city on the other side of the country near the Swiss border. Albert, Hélène, and the others were led from the train and into Switzerland. Across the border they climbed onto another train and were taken to Zürich, then farther east to the border, where they crossed into Constance, Germany. Everything seemed so normal to Albert as he traveled through Switzerland. People went about their daily business, goatherds watched their goats, and small children skipped across train station platforms. It was hard to grasp that Switzerland hadn't been touched by the war.

Constance, Germany, was a stark contrast to Switzerland. Pale, emaciated, listless people stood hopelessly in the city streets begging for food. It was worse than the suffering and starvation Albert had seen in Africa. As soon as they could, Albert and Hélène left Constance behind and headed for Strasbourg, where they were reunited with Hélène's parents.

The next day Albert set out to visit his father. Since Gunsbach was within the sphere of military operations on the German side of the Western Front, he had to get permission to travel there. Once he had a travel permit, he caught a train to Colmar, where the railway line ended because of the war. He would have to walk the last ten miles into the Vosges Mountains to his hometown.

The valley in which Gunsbach nestled was no longer peaceful. In the distance Albert could hear artillery guns roaring from their positions high in the mountains. On the roads, he had to walk between lines of razor wire packed with straw, and everywhere he noticed concrete machine gun emplacements. As he made his way along, he saw houses destroyed by cannon fire, and many of the tree-covered hillsides were now stripped of vegetation. Although Gunsbach was the last inhabited village before the trenches of the Western Front, its location in a valley surrounded by hills had provided enough cover to stop artillery fire from destroying it.

When Albert walked into Gunsbach, he found the streets crowded with wounded German soldiers from the front. He greeted them, but most didn't respond. He could see the indifference in their eyes, as if they'd stopped caring. He found the same indifference in his father's eyes. In the face of danger, his father just sat in his study while artillery shells whistled overhead. He told Albert that he could now barely remember a time when there was no war and no German army officers shared the manse with him.

Albert tried to cheer his father up and care for him, but it was a challenge, given the scarcity of food and other essentials. After several weeks, Hélène obtained permission to travel to Gunsbach. Although she was exhausted from all she'd been through and from her pregnancy, her first job upon arrival was to nurse Albert. He'd hoped the mountain air would cure his dysentery completely, but instead he'd become very sick. A large abscess on his intestine made it difficult for him to even get out of bed. He kept waiting for it to heal, but by late October he realized the abscess needed surgery.

Hélène and Albert supported each other as they started the long walk back to Colmar to get Albert help. They stumbled along for the first two miles until a military wagon picked them up and transported them the rest of the way. In Colmar they stayed the night with Albert's older sister, Louisa, then went by train to Strasbourg, where Albert's old medical lecturer, Professor Stolz, operated on him.

They stayed in Strasbourg while Albert recovered. When word reached the mayor that Albert was there, he visited and offered Albert a job at the city hospital. Albert gladly accepted. At the same time, the Church of St. Nicholas asked Albert back to serve as curate, even offering him the unoccupied parsonage to live in.

On November 11, 1918, the war came to an end with the signing of an armistice between Germany and the Allies. Under the terms of the armistice, Germany was to retreat from all occupied territory in France and Belgium, including Alsace, and remove its forces to the eastern side of the Rhine River. The area of Alsace-Lorraine along the western side of the Rhine was to be annexed by France as it had been before 1871. This brought tremendous upheaval. French forces occupied the area, and all Germans who'd settled there after 1871 were deported back to Germany. This included Hélène's parents, who moved to Heidelberg, leaving seven-months-pregnant Hélène in Strasbourg at a time when she needed their support the most. On the other hand Albert, a descendant of French citizens prior to 1871, was granted French citizenship.

Slowly things began to settle down in Alsace. Families adjusted to the deaths of fathers and husbands during the fighting, rubble was cleared away, and buildings were repaired. Food was still scarce, but Albert knew that his friends in Germany were in worse shape. He often filled a knapsack with food he could spare and walked over the Rhine bridge into Germany to mail it to Richard Wagner's widow, Cosima, and other friends.

A few days before Christmas 1918, Albert received an invitation from Archbishop Nathan Söderblom to come to Sweden after Easter to deliver a series of lectures at the University of Uppsala. At first Albert didn't think he would have the energy to do so, but the archbishop insisted.

On January 14, 1919, Albert's forty-fourth birthday, Hélène gave birth to a daughter whom they named Rhena.

Despite the joy of their new baby, both Hélène and Albert were exhausted and depressed. They decided to go to Sweden and take the baby with them. Archbishop Söderblom invited them to stay at his house. In Sweden, Albert's first lecture at Uppsala University was based on his thoughts regarding reverence for life. He was uplifted by the students' response to it, and his joy returned.

One afternoon as he strolled with Archbishop Söderblom in his beautiful garden, Albert let down his guard. He spoke of his despair at ever returning to Lambaréné. He told the archbishop how he'd borrowed money from the Paris Evangelical Missionary Society and some friends to keep the hospital going, and how he had to pay that all back, as well as raise more money, if he was ever to return. Archbishop Söderblom listened sympathetically and then challenged Albert to have faith. He pointed out that people all over Europe needed to hear Albert's uplifting organ music and lectures. Surely he could give concerts and lectures to raise money. Albert wasn't so sure, but the archbishop insisted it would work. He even offered to set up speaking engagements for Albert. Invigorated by the archbishop's faith in him, Albert took up the challenge.

Archbishop Söderblom was right. Within a year of giving concerts and lectures, Albert had paid off his debts, quit his hospital job, and returned to Gunsbach to be his father's curate. This gave him time to write and plan for his return to Africa. He wrote to the missionary in Lambaréné with whom he'd left his manuscript to have it returned to him. While he awaited its arrival, Albert read through all the newsletters he and Hélène had sent home from Gabon. He edited them into a book and added additional information. The book, *On the Edge of the Primeval Forest,* was published in German, then translated into English, Dutch, French, Danish, and Finnish.

Albert continued giving organ recitals and lectures across Europe, going as far afield as Great Britain and Czechoslovakia. In spring 1923, he completed the first two volumes of *The Philosophy of Civilization,* which were published the same year to much acclaim. Following this, Albert wrote a short book titled *Memoirs of Childhood and Youth* in response to the many questions hundreds of people had asked about his early life.

In February 1924, Albert felt ready to return to Lambaréné. He had used some of his earnings to buy a house in the Black Forest at Königsfeld, Germany. Hélène felt more at home there, especially since it was near the clinic where she was being treated for her ongoing lung condition. Albert and Hélène agreed it would be best for her and five-year-old Rhena to stay there for a while. Albert hoped to get the hospital at Lambaréné up and running again and then return to Hélène and Rhena in Germany to assess what their next step as a family should be.

Chapter 14

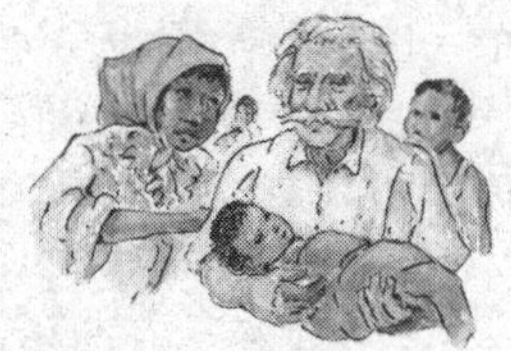

Adolinanango Bantu

On Tuesday, April 15, 1924, Albert once more boarded the paddle steamer *Alémbé* for the trip up the Ogowe River. Noel Gillespie, an eighteen-year-old student from Oxford University, was making the trip with him. Albert had met Noel during a lecture tour of England. Albert had offered to pay Noel's way to Africa if he would go with him to Lambaréné, do some general work at the hospital, and help Albert learn English. Noel had eagerly agreed to go along.

Six years had passed since Albert left Lambaréné, yet as the paddle steamer headed upriver, it seemed to him as though nothing had changed. The vegetation still protruded into the river, making it hard to tell where the jungle ended and river began, while birds still circled overhead and the ever-present monkeys jostled in the treetops. It felt good to be back in Equatorial Africa.

As the *Alémbé* steamed on, Albert chuckled, recalling the customs officer's reaction when he inspected Albert's baggage in Bordeaux before departure. On the voyage, Albert planned to reply to a lot of letters. In fact, he had brought so many letters aboard that they filled four potato sacks. The customs officer frowned as he observed the first sack, then the second. By the time he spotted the fourth sack, he was muttering to himself that he'd never seen anyone travel with so many letters. He then tipped out the first sack and began looking inside each envelope. Albert knew he was looking for French banknotes. It was strictly forbidden for a person to travel outside France carrying more than 5,000 francs. Albert watched for an hour and a half as the officer closely examined the letters one by one. It was a daunting task, and when the officer reached the bottom of the second sack of letters, the he gave up. He let out a deep sigh, shook his head in disbelief, and waved Albert on.

During the voyage Albert worked diligently, writing replies to most of the letters while Noel helped him answer those written in English.

At noon Saturday, Albert and Noel arrived at the hospital at Lambaréné, or at least what was left of it. Even from the river Albert could see it was in terrible disrepair.

The five missionaries currently running the boys' and girls' schools came to meet them. One of the men,

Charles Herrmann, told Albert he'd been able to keep the roofs on the buildings until about a year ago, when they ran out of roof tiles and were unable to procure more because of a labor shortage. After two major exhibits of African wood in Europe, demand was up and the timber trade was booming once more in the Ogowe River Basin. Almost all the available local men were back working for the timber companies and earning top wages.

Back at the mission compound, as if drawn by a magnet, Albert walked up the hill toward his jungle home. The land was so overgrown he could hardly trace the well-trod path that he and Hélène used to follow. His house was smothered in vines, saplings pushed through the floor, and sunlight shone though gaping holes in the roof, but the place was still standing, and inside the house his piano was undamaged.

Next Albert fought his way through the long grass to what remained of the hospital. All that was left was the corrugated iron building housing the consulting room, operating room, dispensary, and sterilizing room. The framework of one of the large raffia-paneled wards still stood. Surveying the scene, Albert knew that his first job was to repair the rotten, leaky roofs of the buildings that were still standing. He and Noel could then tackle the task of reopening the hospital.

That night the sound of drums throbbed across the jungle, carrying the news that the oganga had returned to Lambaréné. Once more, injured and sick people found their way up and down the river to the mission compound. Using the new supply of drugs he had brought with him, Albert treated patients in the mornings and served as building overseer during the afternoons. Because of the labor shortage, he had to make do with "volunteers"—usually family members of patients—who worked unenthusiastically and disappeared from the job whenever Albert wasn't there to cajole them on.

The hospital repair effort received a boost when Emil Ogouma, a local timber merchant, loaned Albert five of his workers for two months until their work contracts ran out. These workers undertook most of the urgent repairs, leaving Albert and Noel free to paddle from village to village begging for roof tiles. Their task was made more difficult because of the prolonged wet season. Albert waited impatiently for the rain to stop, but it just kept falling.

On July 18, 1924, Mathilde Kottman, a nurse from Colmar, arrived to help Albert. It was still raining two months into the supposed dry season, leaving the river flooded and everyone ankle deep in mud. Because of the conditions, the local men couldn't go fishing and crops couldn't be planted. While Albert worried about this situation, he also had personal things to be concerned about. Ulcers had broken out on his legs and feet, making it difficult for him to walk or stand while treating patients. He hadn't experienced this before, and ultimately he had to spend several days in bed waiting for his heavily bandaged legs to stop swelling and for the ulcers to drain.

In August Noel returned to England. Albert was sad to see him go. Noel had been a willing worker, whether he was washing bottles or erecting roof beams. Regrettably, Albert had not had as much time as he would have liked to study English with Noel. Three months after Noel's departure, another helper, Dr. Victor Nessman, a new graduate from medical school, arrived. Albert was delighted. Three medical workers were now at the hospital—two doctors and a nurse, and all from Alsace. Better still, Albert's old friend and former translator, Joseph Azoawani, returned to work at the hospital. Albert welcomed him warmly.

The year 1925 began well in Lambaréné. On January 14 Albert celebrated his fiftieth birthday, and at the end of the month a twenty-eight-foot-long motorboat with a 3.5-horsepower engine chugged up to the mission compound. The vessel was a gift from hospital supporters in Sweden who'd taken up an offering to buy it for the hospital staff. With its shallow draft and narrow beam, the boat was well suited to conditions on the Ogowe River. On its side was painted the name *Tack så mycket,* Swedish for "Many thanks." Albert was grateful for the gift. The boat could carry five people with luggage or twelve without. It also had a long canvas canopy to shield passengers from the sun. Albert looked forward to taking the *Tack så mycket* to bring urgent medical care to villages up and down the river.

Everyone was also thankful when two more workers arrived at Lambaréné—Dr. Mark Lauterburg from Switzerland, and a young widow named Emmy Martin from Alsace. Emmy had been one of Albert's staunchest supporters from the start. She had collected items for use in the hospital and had always helped when crates needed to be packed in Strasbourg for shipment to Africa. While she had no formal medical training, Emmy offered to do whatever necessary to help with hospital administration.

In May 1925 Albert received a letter from his sister in Alsace, informing him that their father had died at age seventy-nine. His father had seemed to lose the will to live after Albert's mother was killed during the war. After hearing the news, Albert thought nostalgically about the family home in Gunsbach. The house belonged to the church, and now another Lutheran pastor and his family would move into the place. It seemed strange to contemplate that Albert no longer had a home to return to in the village he'd loved his whole life. It was the end of an era for him.

Despite his nostalgia, Albert was aware that many things at Lambaréné required his attention. He was grateful when a native carpenter named Monenzali joined the team that was rebuilding and refurbishing the hospital. Monenzali had learned carpentry at Cape Lopez and was a skilled worker. His efficient and steady work habits began to rub off on some of the local workers, much to Albert's delight.

At last everything seemed to be going well, and Albert looked forward to devoting his evenings to reading and writing. But as the unrelenting summer heat began, twin disasters struck the Ogowe region.

The first was an epidemic. At the start a few people from upriver timber camps began showing up at the hospital with stomach cramps, vomiting, and bloody diarrhea. Since these were common symptoms of tropical illnesses, Albert took samples of body fluids and studied them under his microscope. He detected the thin strands of bacteria that were the telltale sign of dysentery.

With the discovery, Albert knew that the medical staff needed to act quickly. Dysentery was incredibly contagious, and without fast action, it would spread throughout the hospital. To combat the disease, people throughout the local area were encouraged to drink and cook with boiled water. But old habits proved hard to break, and many people continued using unboiled river water. It was frustrating when someone came to the hospital with a different illness, only to end up catching dysentery and dying. *Would it be better if we closed the hospital down altogether?* Albert pondered, though he knew that wasn't the answer.

The dysentery epidemic finally subsided, but not before killing thousands of people. Then a second disaster loomed. Since locals had been unable to plant crops during the extended wet season the year before, food staples were in short supply. Albert had foreseen this and stockpiled as much rice as possible at the hospital. This supply was used to feed the medical staff and supplement the patients' diets. The locals were also depending on rice, which they procured from merchants, as their main food staple. But when a ship carrying thousands of tons of rice destined for the area was shipwrecked and the rice ruined, the merchants had no more rice to sell, and hunger and famine spread. Albert did what he could to help, using the *Tack så mycket* to transport as much rice to the local villages as he could spare.

French schoolteacher Emma Haussknecht arrived at Lambaréné in October 1925 to assist Emmy Martin with hospital administration. This brought the total number of European hospital staff to six. With three extra women the hospital began accepting newborn babies who had nowhere else to go. Twins born in Gabon were particularly vulnerable. Many people believed a mother could only pass her spirit to one child, which meant that in the case of twins, one baby was obviously an evil imposter. Since no one could tell which twin was which, both were often cast aside to die. The babies of mothers who died giving birth or soon after often met a similar fate. Witch doctors called orphaned babies cursed, and no other mother wanted to take on the role of breastfeeding a cursed newborn. Thankfully, a new product, canned evaporated milk, could be bottle-fed to babies to keep them alive. Albert ordered a shipment of evaporated milk from France, and the women at the hospital took on the task of bottle-feeding and saving the lives of the babies left with them.

By late 1925, the hospital was completely rebuilt, along with a ward for European patients. This meant that Albert no longer had to give up his bedroom when a timber merchant or missionary needed ongoing medical attention. The hospital even had two small cells to house people so mentally tormented they were a danger to themselves and their families. Before coming to Africa, Albert hadn't considered the possibility that native people would struggle with mental illness. He soon discovered it was a grim fact of life for them. His first encounter with an African person with mental illness was N'Tschambi, a giant of a man. He had been delivered to the hospital in chains, and Albert was informed he'd killed his wife with an ax in a fit of rage. If the hospital did not take him, Albert knew N'Tschambi would be killed by those from his village. In time, N'Tschambi recovered and could be trusted to do tasks around the hospital during the day, but he was locked in his room at night.

With the dysentery and famine behind him, Albert took a canoe trip on the river to pray and think about things. The dysentery epidemic had made clear to him the necessity for the hospital to be enlarged. It needed a ward in which to quarantine those with infectious diseases, and there was also a desperate need for more housing for the mentally ill. The problem was that no more land was available at the mission school compound at Lambaréné. The hospital was surrounded by water, swamp, and steep hills. And although he knew it would be challenge, Albert became convinced he needed to build a new hospital on a larger, better suited parcel of land.

The site Albert sought for his new hospital needed to be on the river, since there were no roads in the area. Preferably it would be near the Big Island so that supplies could be delivered more easily, and it needed to be a large, flat piece of land where Albert could develop a village around the hospital.

Albert found the land he was looking for a mile and a half upriver from the mission compound. The area was called Adolinanango Bantu, which means "looking out over the people." It was a flat-topped hill beside the river on the opposite bank from the Catholic mission station on the Big island. Long ago, Albert learned, a large village had stood on the site, and N'Kombe, "the Sun King," had lived there. During this time the land around the village was cleared and cultivated. After the village was abandoned, the first European trader in the area, a colorful Englishman named Alfred Aloysius Smith, who went by the nickname Trader Horn, built a house and lived on the site. He too cultivated the land and planted many fruit trees, which were rare in that part of Gabon.

As he walked around the land pondering the possibilities, Albert was struck by the enormity of the task before him. Building a new hospital on a new site would require a great deal of money, labor, and materials, all of which were in short supply. Not only that—he knew that if he embarked on the project, he wouldn't be able to reunite with Hélène and Rhena as planned. Yet he knew in his heart that building a new and bigger hospital was the right thing to do. He would have to wait until the new hospital was complete before returning to Europe. Albert visited the district commissioner and asked to be granted land at the new site to build the hospital. He expected it to be a long, drawn-out negotiation, but much to his surprise, the commissioner immediately agreed to give Albert 172 acres of the land as a concession for the hospital.

Now that he had permission to use the land, Albert sent workers, the friends and family members of patients he was treating, to clear it in preparation for building. He left as many trees as possible in place to provide shade. Soon the workers freed the papaya and mango trees and the oil palms from the vines slowly choking them. These trees were strong and mature, and Albert knew that with care they would provide plenty of fruit for the hospital.

As work began at the new site, Dr. Victor Nessman returned to France to undertake his compulsory military service. He was replaced by Dr. Frédéric Trenz from Strasbourg. Albert continued to alternate between treating patients at the hospital in the morning and supervising the building of the new hospital in the afternoon. Regarding his work at the new site, Albert noted in a letter home,

> No great demands are being made on my intellect. I drive in the piles for pile houses, clear the jungle, direct excavations, supervise the lay of floors, try to figure out the best locations for laundry rooms and toilets, hunt for a satisfactory place for rain runoff, pick up crates from the river steamer.

Albert gradually spent more and more of his time supervising the building project. He ordered building materials from Strasbourg, including corrugated iron for roofs and walls. At the same time, many donations, both large and small, came in designated for the new hospital. One large donation came from the staff of a Bible publishing house in Japan. Albert had no idea how they'd heard about his work in the jungle of Gabon, but he was grateful for their sacrifice.

As he worked on construction, Albert received a letter from Hélène, telling him her father had died in Germany. Albert wished he could be there to comfort his wife and honor a man whom he'd greatly admired, but it was not possible.

Building supplies began arriving from France and other places, and soon the buildings were taking shape. By early 1927 some of the structures were finished, and on January 21, patients began being transferred from the old to the new hospital. Albert wrote to his supporters describing the move.

> On the evening of the last journey we made, I took the mental patients with me. Their guardians never tired of telling them that in the new hospital they would live in cells with wood floors. In the old cells the floor had been just the damp earth. When I made my tour of the hospital that evening, there resounded from every fire and every mosquito net the greeting "It's a good hut, Doctor, a very good hut!" So now for the first time since I began to work

in Africa fourteen years ago my patients were housed as human beings should be.

Three months later, Lilian Russell arrived at Lambaréné. She was the widow of a well-known youth club movement leader in England and the daughter of an English diplomat to Zanzibar, General Christopher Rigby. She spoke German and French fluently, but as far as Albert was concerned, her main asset was her uncanny ability to get the native people to follow her directions. Albert mapped out a plan for an extensive garden and orchard around the hospital and left the responsibility for making it happen in Lilian's capable hands. This allowed Albert to complete the building of several additional wards. By mid-1927 the hospital could accommodate two hundred patients along with those who accompanied them.

A church in London, England, sent enough money to build a ward specifically for mental patients. When construction of this building was complete, Albert felt at liberty to book passage on a ship back to Europe, leaving the responsibility for running the hospital in the hands of capable colleagues.

On July 21, 1927, Albert caught a paddle steamer at Lambaréné and headed downriver for Cape Lopez, where he wearily boarded a ship. He had been in Africa for three and a half long years and desperately wanted to see his wife and daughter again.

Chapter 15

The Madness of These Nations

Albert realized he'd been away a long time when he saw the tall girl with long, dark pigtails running down the path toward him. It was his eight-year-old daughter, Rhena. She smiled, showing her new front teeth as Albert enveloped her in a hug. It was good to be in Königsfeld, Germany, with his wife and daughter again. That night, and many nights after, Albert and Hélène sat and talked after dinner in their simple house. They had so much to tell each other and many things to discuss regarding all that needed to be done during Albert's furlough.

When word got around that Albert Schweitzer was back in Königsfeld, invitations poured in for him to give lectures and concerts. Albert tried to accept as many of these as he could. He hoped they would help his goal of telling people what was happening at the new hospital at Lambaréné so that he could recruit more workers for it and raise funds to keep it all going. Hélène accompanied Albert as much as possible to these events, sometimes serving as his English translator. Albert still found communicating in English challenging. Together they traveled to Holland to give a pipe organ concert for the Dutch queen mother, and to Oxford University in England, where Albert gave a series of lectures on religion. When back in Königsfeld, Albert worked on the new book he was writing.

One year into his furlough, Albert learned that he'd been awarded the Goethe Prize for "services to humanity," for which he received 10,000 Deutsche marks as prize money. It was a great honor. Albert decided to use the money for a project he'd been dreaming of since his father's death—a permanent home in Gunsbach, not just for himself but as a headquarters for the work in Lambaréné. It would be a place where hospital workers could stay on furlough and where items could be gathered and shipped to Gabon. Emmy Martin, who'd returned from Lambaréné, agreed to run the house and represent the hospital's needs in France. Albert designed the building himself and took great delight in watching its construction. How much easier it was to get things built in Alsace!

By the end of Albert's second year of furlough, the Gunsbach house was complete and Emmy had moved in. Rhena was attending a Moravian boarding school nearby, and Albert felt it was time for him to return to Lambaréné, accompanied by his wife. Hélène's health had been up and down as usual during Albert's time home, but she was determined to go with him to Africa. In early December 1929, they set sail from Bordeaux for Cape Lopez aboard the *Amérique*. Traveling with them were nurse Marie Secretan, employed to be Hélène's traveling companion in case she became sick at sea, and Anna Schmitz, a German doctor who'd volunteered to serve at the hospital. As usual, Albert had writing supplies with him on the voyage so that he could work on the autobiography he'd started writing. So many people had requested it that he felt he should continue working on it.

The voyage south didn't go well. Hélène became so ill that Albert wondered if he should send her and Marie straight back to Europe. But Hélène had set her heart on seeing the new hospital, and after all the sacrifices she'd made to support it, Albert couldn't deny her.

The day after Christmas 1929, Albert and Hélène disembarked the riverboat. A large group of cheering Africans and Europeans stood on the riverbank to welcome them back to Lambaréné. They were accompanied up the rise to the dining room, where Albert proudly showed Hélène the way it was designed with ventilation in the rafters. By the time dinner was over, Hélène was tired. She leaned heavily on Albert's arm as he led her to their new home.

The following morning Albert took Hélène on a detailed tour of the hospital and grounds. He was delighted to see how well things had progressed during his two-year absence. Lilian Russell had done a wonderful job with the gardens, and each day heaping bowls of oranges, grapefruit, tangerines, and pineapple were served at lunch. In addition, the patients and their families were also receiving rice, manioc, and green bananas daily.

Although he was now fifty-four years old, Albert felt invigorated. As he settled back into the hospital routine, Hélène would spend hours sitting on the veranda of their home, spending time with nurses and patients. She also worked diligently editing the pages of Albert's autobiography. However, after five months at Lambaréné, it was obvious that her health wasn't improving. The extreme climate caused a resurgence of her tuberculosis. In May 1930 Hélène returned to a sanatorium in Germany to recuperate.

While in Europe, Albert had designed a new hospital operating room, which he began constructing after Hélène's departure. He had brought back all the necessary medical equipment for it, which had been donated by supporters of the hospital. To Albert this was amazing, given the fact that the United States and most countries in Europe had plunged into an economic depression just prior to his return to Africa.

Albert received regular letters from Hélène throughout her nine-month stay at the sanatorium in the Black Forest near Königsfeld. He was grateful both for her restored health and for her willingness to guide his autobiography to publication. The book was published in 1931 under the title *Out of My Life and Thought*. And with the book's publication, more mail began piling up for Albert to answer.

In early January 1932, Albert left Lambaréné once more to return to Europe. He hated the thought of arriving there in midwinter, but he had accepted an invitation to be the keynote speaker on March 22 in Frankfurt, Germany, at the centennial of the death of Goethe, the highly celebrated German literary figure. Hélène and thirteen-year-old Rhena joined him there. At the exact hour of Goethe's death one hundred years before, Albert began his keynote address.

Two months after the address in Frankfurt, Albert set off for Great Britain, where he was showered with honors. He returned home with four honorary doctorate degrees from the universities at Oxford, St. Andrews, and Edinburgh.

In January 1933, Albert was in Berlin when Adolf Hitler was named chancellor of Germany by President Paul von Hindenburg. Albert was appalled at this turn of events. As far as he was concerned, Hitler and his Nazi party were bullies who were systematically undermining civil order in Germany. In a letter to Hélène, who was in Gunsbach with Rhena, Albert wrote,

> Oh, I suffer terribly from these times, I am completely without hope. What will all of this lead to . . . The situation in France. In Germany Hitler is seizing the reins. They were such dreadful days for me in Berlin. . . . In these days the last chance of improving relations

> was relinquished . . . God help us out of this. . . . Every day I have to tear myself out of this sadness in order to get to work. . . . Before a new spirit can arise, the madness of these nations will have destroyed everything that still stands.

By now Albert was aware of the Nazis' hatred for Jews, who had become the scapegoats for everything wrong in Germany. Everywhere he went, he urged Jewish people to find a way to get out of the country. Hélène's older brother, Ernst Bresslau, was a well-known professor at the University of Cologne, where he had helped found the zoology department. When Ernst was fired from his university position for being Jewish, Albert agreed to help pay the passage to Brazil for Ernst, his wife, and their four children, and to support them once they settled in São Paulo. He was relieved that his brother-in-law and his family were getting out of Germany while they could. He hoped that many other Jews followed.

In March 1933, Albert left France for Africa aboard the M.V. *Brazza.* His heart was heavy despite all the support and recognition he'd received for the hospital. The events occurring in Germany troubled Albert greatly. He sensed things wouldn't end well, and feared that Europe might once again be plunged into a bloody war.

Back in Lambaréné, Albert was cheered by the accomplishments of his staff. Each doctor had performed over five hundred surgeries, and donations from Albert's relatives and a doctor friend had been enough to purchase a gas-powered refrigerator. Now each morning and afternoon, a glass of cold water was delivered to each doctor and nurse to refresh them as they went about their duties. Albert was also delighted to see that seventy breadfruit tree saplings had been planted on the grounds. It would take several years for them to mature, but when they did, their fruit would help feed patients.

However, Albert's joy over the hospital's progress was fleeting. He received an urgent letter from Hélène stating that the Nazi party was beginning to tighten control over Jewish people. Although Hélène had converted to Christianity, the Nazis considered her Jewish by birth and blocked her bank account. Also, the Jewish doctor providing her ongoing tuberculosis treatment was fired, and she couldn't find another doctor in Germany willing to treat her. She could only imagine things getting worse for her, and she informed Albert that she and Rhena were moving to Switzerland at the end of the school year.

The following year, in late 1934, Albert again returned to Europe and based himself in Gunsbach. He visited Hélène and Rhena in Lausanne, Switzerland, and Hélène traveled with him to England and Scotland. In Edinburgh, Scotland, Albert gave a series of lectures that were published in an American magazine. Although the British welcomed Albert warmly, he was saddened that many of his German clergy friends asked him not to visit them. They didn't want to associate with someone who was speaking out against Hitler and the Nazis. After receiving the letters, Albert vowed never to set foot in Germany again while Adolf Hitler was in power. And when Joseph Goebbels, the Nazi minister of propaganda, wrote asking Albert to publicly endorse Adolf Hitler, Albert sent back a scathing reply stating all the reasons he would never do such a thing. Given Hitler's ambitions for Europe and the brutal actions of the Nazis, Albert felt that war and bloodshed in Europe were inevitable, and he wanted to stay as far away from them as possible.

In Switzerland, with great public fanfare, people insisted on celebrating Albert's sixtieth birthday on January 14, 1935. Albert and Hélène spent a week in a Swiss village on the shores of Lake Geneva before it was time for Albert to return to Lambaréné once more.

In May, back in Lambaréné, Albert learned that tragedy had struck the Bresslau family. Hélène's older brother, Ernst, had died of a heart attack in Brazil. Albert was convinced that the stress of being fired from his job and having to flee Germany had contributed to his death. Albert sent money he'd earned giving concerts in Europe to Ernst's family in São Paulo to help with financial support.

In mid-December 1935, Albert was back in England, making a series of organ recordings for Columbia Records. He was playing Bach's music on the organ at All Hallows by the Tower in London. At first he wasn't satisfied with the quality of the recordings. Albert felt that the sound was muffled and lacked the musical clarity he sought. To rectify the situation, he suggested the microphones be changed and repositioned. Two small diaphragm condenser microphones were pointed directly away from each other so that the sound information each microphone captured was unique. A large diaphragm condenser microphone was then placed above and pointed directly at the organ. Albert was pleased with the new microphone arrangement, which produced a much clearer sound recording. The sound engineers doing the recording dubbed Albert's microphone arrangement the Schweitzer Technique.

Over the next three years Albert watched as turmoil grew in Europe and other parts of the world. Hitler gained more influence over Germany, and persecution of Jews there continued to grow. Italy's brutal invasion and occupation of Ethiopia, an East African country, began in 1935 and continued until May 7, 1936, when Italy annexed the country. In 1936, Italian leader Benito Mussolini and Adolf Hitler joined together to give their support to Francisco Franco and his Nationalist forces in the civil war that had broken out in Spain. This in turn led to a treaty of cooperation between Italy and Germany on foreign policy. In July 1937 in Far East Asia, Japan invaded China, and on March 12, 1938, Adolf Hitler annexed his home country of Austria into Germany. Several months later, Germany also annexed Sudetenland, the German name for the northern, southern, and western areas of Czechoslovakia inhabited by Germans.

As these events played out, Albert became convinced that another war was coming and that it would be a long one—perhaps seven years in length. As a result, he spent many weeks working on plans to keep the hospital open and supplied with food and medicine. The traders at Cape Lopez believed that if there was another war in Europe, they would still be able to import rice and other goods from China. Because of this, they were willing to sell Albert huge quantities of weevil-infested rice. Albert doubted the traders' optimism. Things were not particularly stable in Far East Asia. With the Japanese having already overrun China, no one was sure about their intentions for the rest of the region. That was why Albert believed that if war did come, it wouldn't just be in Europe but across the world. Nonetheless, he bought every grain of rice the traders offered him. Weevil-infested rice might not sound appealing now, but Albert knew that it could be the difference between starvation and survival for many people.

With a heavy heart, Albert also began streamlining hospital procedures. Only those patients who were seriously ill and would benefit from hospital care were allowed to remain. Others with long-term illnesses that had no cure were sent home to their villages. Many of the staff also left as the situation in Europe became more unstable. Albert was grateful that Dr. Ladislas Goldschmid, a Hungarian specialist in elephantiasis who'd been at Lambaréné for six years, agreed to stay. Three nurses, two Swiss and one Dutch, also committed to stay, along with two other female Swiss workers, Albert's two loyal administrative assistants, Emma Haussknecht and Mathilde Kottmann.

During this time Albert also received news that Charles Widor had died in March 1937 at the age of ninety-three. While the news saddened him, Albert realized that his old pipe organ tutor and mentor had lived a full and interesting life pursing his passion for music.

Albert made another trip to Europe in January 1939. He intended to stay several months and await Hélène and Rhena's return from the United States, where Hélène was lecturing about the medical mission work at Lambaréné. At each port where the ship stopped on the voyage to Europe, Albert noticed German warships docked or at anchor. As Albert's ship approached France, Hitler's speech to the German Reichstag was broadcast via radio on January 30. Albert hung his head in sorrow as he listened. Although Hitler vowed to German legislators and the world that he had no further plans to dominate Europe, Albert didn't believe a word the man said. In fact, he was more convinced than ever that war was imminent.

After docking in Bordeaux, Albert knew he couldn't spend a day longer in Europe than necessary. He had to get back to his hospital before war broke out. The ship he arrived on had a ten-day turnaround time before embarking on the return trip to Africa. Albert decided that was long enough to acquire as many medicines and canned goods as he possibly could. He booked a return ticket on the same vessel and wrote a hasty letter to Hélène informing her of his change of plans. He then headed to Gunsbach, where he worked around the clock to contact supporters and gather medicines and canned milk. Back in Bordeaux ten days later, Albert purchased a gas-powered lamp, which would allow the doctors to perform emergency surgeries at night at the hospital. He then boarded the ship and said farewell to Europe. He wondered if or when he would ever see it again, and if so, in what condition it would be.

Four months after Albert's hasty trip to France, Hélène and Rhena arrived at Lambaréné. Albert was proud to show his twenty-year-old daughter around the hospital, as she'd never seen his work in Gabon. Rhena also had news for Albert. She was engaged to Jean Eckert, an organ builder from Paris. Albert was happy for them, but he couldn't help but worry about their future in Europe, since Jean was Jewish.

After a six-week visit, Hélène and Rhena returned to Paris. Hélène wanted to check on her mother and then arrange a small wedding for Rhena and Jean. She felt confident that their French passports would protect them from political harm. Albert wasn't so sure.

Chapter 16

War Comes to Lambaréné

Albert was right. He hadn't believed a word Adolf Hitler had said during his Reichstag speech back in January about having no further plans to dominate Europe. Now on September 3, 1939, Albert sat in silence, rereading the bulletin sent to the hospital from the French colonial representative in Lambaréné. He had been predicting that this day would come for a long time. Yet now that it was here, it was difficult to believe that European countries would plunge themselves into all-out war just twenty-one years after the previous one. Two days before, Hitler had launched a massive and brutal invasion of neighboring Poland. Now Britain and France had declared war on Germany in defense of Poland. As far as Albert was concerned, it was only a matter of time before all of Europe and the world would be involved.

Albert's thoughts turned to Hélène—where was she now?—and to Rhena and her husband, Jean Eckert, who were expecting their first child. As a Jewish family, would they be safe? And what about his brother Paul's two sons? Nineteen-year-old Jean-Jacques had already joined the French Marines, and twenty-seven-year-old Pierre-Paul would undoubtedly be conscripted. Would they be killed? Albert was overwhelmed by the images of young men dying, lives being wasted, ancient buildings being ruined, and land being destroyed.

Although radio transmission capabilities had come to Lambaréné the year before, and several hospital staff members had radios, Albert had refused to buy one for the hospital. He knew that many depressing months of war news lay ahead. He decided it was enough for him to receive semiweekly updates from the French colonial representative, although even that might prove too much for him.

Albert was grateful that at least the hospital had a large supply of rice and canned evaporated milk, and that a large shipment of medicines he'd purchased in France was awaiting shipment to Gabon. He was also grateful that Dr. Ladislas Goldschmid had kept his promise to remain at Lambaréné for the duration of the war and that Dr. Anna Wildikann, who had previously been with the hospital for two years, had written saying she was working at finding a way back to the hospital from her native Latvia. Albert was relieved to see her when she arrived safely at Lambaréné on January 11, 1940. Toward the end of the month, Gertrude Koch, a Swiss nurse, returned home after her third period of work at the hospital. This brought the total number of European medical workers to three doctors and four nurses. Two nurses were Swiss, one was Dutch, and the fourth was from Alsace. Sadly, one of Albert's long-serving workers, nurse Mathilde Kottman, had been on furlough in Strasbourg and was unable to get back to the hospital before war broke out.

On May 10, 1940, the Germans began an offensive against France, Belgium, the Netherlands, and Luxembourg. Sixteen days later, the hospital at Lambaréné felt the direct impact of the war in Europe. The M.V. *Brazza*, the ocean liner Albert had sailed on many times between Bordeaux and French Equatorial Africa, was torpedoed by a German submarine near Cape Finisterre on the north coast of Spain while making her way south to Africa. The ship sank quickly, and 378 of the 575 people aboard died. This came as a blow to Albert, who knew many of the crew, including the captain, aboard the *Brazza*. Also devastating was the loss of a large shipment, in the cargo hold of the torpedoed ship, of drugs and other materials for the hospital. Now the supplies were at the bottom of the Atlantic Ocean with the remains of the ship. Albert's worst fears had been confirmed. As during the first war, Gabon would be cut off from European supplies.

The twice-weekly news bulletins Albert received reported that the Germans had moved decisively. By early June they breached the French defensive line and marched into Paris. The French government abandoned the city to the Nazis and fled to Bordeaux, while the Italians attacked southeast France. In the end, the French government signed an armistice with Germany on June 22, 1940. Albert shook his head as he read the bulletin outlining the terms of the armistice. France was now divided into occupied and unoccupied zones. The occupied zone covered the north and west of the country, including the entire Atlantic coast, and was controlled by the Germans. A small zone in the southeast was occupied by the Italians.

The unoccupied zone consisted of the remaining two-fifths of the country in the south. This was known as *zone libre*, or the free zone, and would be governed by France's new and officially neutral government led by Marshal Philippe Pétain. His government was based in the city of Vichy in central France, 190 miles south of Paris. The Vichy government was also in charge of many of the civil functions in the northern zone as well as of French colonial territories in North and Equatorial Africa and Southeast Asia.

Albert felt sick reading the report. This new Vichy government was nothing more than a German puppet state, yet there was a glimmer of hope for France. French General Charles de Gaulle, who'd been a government minister, rejected the armistice with Germany and fled to Great Britain, where he established a government in exile known as Free France. General de Gaulle also established the Free French Forces to continue fighting against Germany and to organize and support the resistance in occupied France. He broadcast a radio address over the BBC to all French citizens, exhorting them to resist the Germans and the Vichy government, and urging French military forces stationed in French colonies around the world to give their allegiance to Free France.

The turmoil in France resulted in Albert's losing contact with many of his friends and relatives, including his daughter, Rhena, who as far as he knew was still in Paris with her husband and new baby daughter, Monique. And where was Hélène? He didn't know. Nor did he know how Gunsbach—let alone any members of his family there—was faring.

Before long, though, Albert had war concerns much closer to the hospital that he had to contend with. By the end of August 1940, all of French Equatorial Africa except Gabon had pledged allegiance to Free France. Soon afterward General de Gaulle came to the region to solidify support for Free France and deal with the situation in Gabon. On October 27, Free French Forces crossed into Gabon from the north. They quickly took control of the town of Mitzic and moved south, turning their attention to the garrison at Lambaréné, which was controlled by soldiers loyal to the Vichy government.

Albert became aware of the encroaching battle when airplanes belonging to the Free French Forces thundered low over the hospital as they approached the Lambaréné garrison across the river. As gunshots and explosions rang out across the Ogowe, Albert and his staff worked hurriedly to reinforce the wooden walls of buildings facing Lambaréné with thick sheets of corrugated iron. Soon, frightened European and African residents of the Lambaréné township made their way over the river by boat or canoe to seek refuge at the hospital. Albert welcomed them. The battle was fierce and loud, and wounded soldiers from both sides were carried to the hospital, where they were treated equally with the best medical care possible.

On November 5, the Vichy-controlled garrison surrendered to the Free French troops, and the fighting moved on. Calm once more descended over Lambaréné.

Seven days later, on November 12, 1940, Free French forces took complete control of Gabon. Now all of French Equatorial Africa was in the hands of Free France and cooperating with the Allies. This meant that all shipments to and from France and most of Europe were canceled. This had a devastating effect on the local economy in Gabon. Exports of timber, coffee, cocoa, and palm oil came to an abrupt halt. And although shipping lanes to the United States remained open, the main commodity the Americans wanted from Africa was rubber now that the Dutch East Indies, their previous rubber supplier, had been captured by the Japanese.

As he contemplated how the hospital would fare now that they were cut off from Europe, Albert received some good news. It came in the form of two letters from Christian groups in the United States who had heard about Albert's work at the hospital from Hélène. The groups offered to fund and send whatever drugs and equipment the hospital needed to keep it running while the war went on. A third letter from the United States informed him that the Albert Schweitzer Fellowship had been established, also because of Hélène's influence. The fellowship existed to raise awareness and funds for the hospital in Lambaréné.

On August 2, 1941, a most unexpected thing happened. The drums began beating out across the jungle. Their message relayed that Hélène Schweitzer was arriving via motorcar. Albert could scarcely believe it. His wife was coming by car up the new road the Allies were building from the top to the bottom of Africa. Currently the road ended on the southern bank of the Ogowe River. Albert sent some local men in a canoe to await Hélène's arrival and bring her safely to the hospital.

Just before midnight the next day, Albert stood at the landing spot beside the river waiting for his wife. It seemed like a miracle when the canoe appeared in the darkness and Hélène stepped from it. Her hair was gray, and she looked gaunt, but she was alive and standing before him.

The following day Albert heard all about Hélène's struggles. Although she'd gone back to live in Switzerland after her six-week visit to Lambaréné in 1939, she had been visiting Rhena and Jean and baby

Monique in Paris when the Germans marched into the city. This prompted a mass exodus of Parisians before the Nazis officially took control of the city. Hélène and the Eckert family fled along with more than two million others and headed to the south of France, where they lived together in a hotel.

Hélène described how, during this time, she felt she had to get to Albert and was able to escape France and make her way to Lisbon, Portugal, where she boarded a ship bound for Angola. Upon arrival in Angola she hired a car and driver to take her north on the newly built road through the Belgian Congo to Brazzaville and then to the south bank of the Ogowe River. It had been a harrowing trip for her and, as far as Albert was concerned, a heroic one.

Hélène also had more news to tell Albert. She wasn't sure what had happened to Rhena. She did know that Rhena and Jean had hoped to escape to Switzerland with their baby, and that Rhena was expecting another child near the end of the year. All Albert could do was pray they had made it to Switzerland before they were rounded up by the Nazis.

Once Hélène recovered from the exhausting trip, she announced to Albert that she was ready to work. And work she did, relieving each of the hospital's nurses in shifts so that they could take much-needed breaks. Albert was relieved to have Hélène at his side again. He valued her wisdom and long history with the hospital.

On December 8, 1941, the day after a Japanese aerial attack on the American Pacific Fleet anchored at Pearl Harbor, Hawaii, the United States declared war on Japan. Three days later, it also declared war on Germany and Italy. Many people thought this would bring a fast end to the war, but Albert was not so optimistic. War raged around the world, from Asia and the Pacific to Europe and North Africa. Albert didn't think the addition of one more combatant would bring the war to a speedy end. He had always thought a war like this would last at least seven years, and right now they were just over two years in.

In early 1942, a shipment arrived from the United States for the hospital. Albert and the hospital staff cried tears of joy as they unpacked the boxes containing thermos flasks, household utensils, gardening tools, the latest medicines, and something that made Albert particularly happy—large-sized rubber gloves. For the previous six months he'd been squeezing his hands into small gloves when performing surgery.

Now Albert looked around with renewed hope, and he saw an opportunity. He had money from the United States, a supply of tools and equipment, and many able-bodied workers without jobs. It was time to do the projects on the hospital grounds he'd put off doing. A strong stone wall along the shoreline was needed to protect the land from floods, the "streets" around the hospital needed paving, and Albert could envisage enlarging the orchards and gardens. He rearranged his workdays as he had many times before, performing surgeries and seeing patients in the mornings and supervising work crews in the afternoons. It was amazing to him how quickly the improvements were made. Albert personally planted one thousand orange and grapefruit seeds, tended them as they sprouted, and then transplanted the seedlings into the orchard. It reminded him of the days as a boy when he had tended his father's grapevines on the slopes above Gunsbach.

Very occasionally news reached Albert and Hélène about their family and friends. Rhena had given birth to two more children, a son named Philippe and a daughter, Christiane. The family was "safe" in Switzerland, as much as anyone was safe during the wretched war. Hélène was sad to learn that her favorite cousin, Johanna Engel, had committed suicide in Germany rather than be sent to a concentration camp. Albert's nephew, Pierre-Paul Schweitzer, who worked for the French Underground, had been captured and was now imprisoned in the Buchenwald concentration camp. Hélène's mother had died, as had Albert's brother-in-law, Albert Woytt. And an Allied bomb had hit the building in Strasbourg where Fritz Munch, Ernst's son, and his family had sought shelter. Fritz's wife and two of their children were killed in the blast. Albert despaired. Would there be any end to the killing?

On January 14, 1945, Albert turned seventy. The war still raged on, and he didn't feel much like celebrating. Nonetheless, he'd received word that the BBC in England was to broadcast a special radio program in his honor. A European woman who had taken shelter at the hospital when her husband was conscripted into the army had a portable radio, and the hospital staff gathered in her room to listen to the broadcast. Dr. Micklem, a theologian from Oxford University, discussed the theories contained in Albert's book *The Quest of the Historic Jesus,* and then they aired a recording of Albert playing Bach on the organ. Albert held back tears as he listened to the organ recording, made so many years before and so many miles away. When the radio broadcast was over, everyone was silent for several minutes before filing out of the room.

Later that day Albert wrote a letter to the members of the General Council of Congregational Churches in the United States, thanking them for their generosity in financially supporting the work of the hospital at Lambaréné. In the letter he noted, "For what I have to do and for a long time, it might be good for the hospital if I could go on directing it. I ought to be thirty and not seventy years old. But it is a great privilege that at seventy I am able to do the necessary [work]."

It was Monday, May 7, 1945, and as usual, Albert spent the morning treating patients. At lunchtime he stopped to write some letters, hoping that a riverboat would arrive to take them downriver. As he sat at his desk writing, he looked up to see a European patient grinning at him through the open window. "Monsieur Le Grand Docteur, the war in Europe is over. I just heard it on the radio. Germany has surrendered."

Albert nodded and continued to write. After so many years of turmoil in the world, he found it hard to take in the news. The war was over? Really over? It was difficult for Albert to process the idea.

Later that afternoon, Albert rang the bell to call everyone into the central courtyard of the hospital. There he announced to all that the war in Europe was over. Germany had unconditionally surrendered at the Allied headquarters in Reims, France. Albert then said a brief prayer of thanks before they all returned to their work. So many lives had been lost in the war, so much evil had been done, and so many futures had been ruined that he could not celebrate. No person who had a reverence for life could.

Chapter 17

Le Grand Docteur

Three years after the end of World War II, Albert was able to return to Europe. By that time, the doctors and nurses who had faithfully served at the hospital through the war had either gone on leave or finished their service at Lambaréné, and Albert had welcomed and oriented three new doctors and six nurses. There had also been the struggle of another famine that had caused food prices to skyrocket to four times what they'd been. There were breakthroughs too, one of which was the new "wonder drug," penicillin. It had been widely used for the first time during the war to treat soldiers with infections. Now for the first time in history, there was a way to save the lives of hundreds of thousands of people who would have previously died from various infections. Albert was delighted when the first shipment of penicillin arrived in Lambaréné and he could put the new drug to the test. It worked like a miracle.

By the time Albert and Hélène arrived back in Gunsbach in October 1948, Albert was ready for a long rest. He'd been in Lambaréné for twelve years, except for his hurried ten days in Europe to gather supplies in early 1939. As usual, it was a rest Albert never got. Many people were waiting to meet him. Journalists, doctors, pastors, and university lecturers were clamoring to interview him or have him speak. Albert's opinion was sought on everything from pipe organ design to the latest breakthroughs in surgery. Albert found himself honored with parades, speeches, the presentation of keys to cities, and many other honors. It seemed Albert stood out as a beacon of hope for a better future in war-ravaged France.

As soon as they could after their arrival in Europe, Hélène and Albert journeyed to Zurich, Switzerland, to see Rhena, Jean, and their four grandchildren. Albert met Monique, Philippe, Christiane, and Catherine for the first time. The ages of the children ranged from nine down to four, and Albert thought each child was wonderful. The children were bright and curious, with the older ones already excelling at their piano lessons. Soon after arriving, Albert, acting in his role as pastor, baptized all four grandchildren in the living room. Rhena and Jean had been looking forward to his being able to do that.

While in France, Albert was invited to give the keynote address at the bicentenary of Goethe's birth, which was to be held in Aspen, Colorado, in the United States. Dignitaries and scholars from around the world would be there. At first Albert turned down the invitation, feeling he needed to get back to Lambaréné. When asked to reconsider, he thought more about it. Just as he was about to decide, the Goethe organization offered to add a donation of $5,000 for the hospital to the $5,000 they would pay as his speaking fee. Albert couldn't turn down the invitation a second time. While in the United States, he could also learn more about the new sulfone drugs dapsone and promin, which were being used to treat leprosy. With the hospital donation, he could buy a good supply of the drugs and still return to Lambaréné with enough money to start his next project, a village for leprosy patients. Although he was now seventy-four years old and Hélène was seventy and in poor health, the opportunity to go to North America was too good to turn down. Hundreds of sick Africans would benefit from it.

The Schweitzers arrived in New York aboard the liner *Nieuw Amsterdam* on June 28, 1949. At the bottom of the gangway they were met by a crowd of reporters yelling over each other to ask Albert questions. Some of the questions struck Albert as funny. One reporter asked, "Tell me, Doctor, what do you think of America?" Albert smiled and said, "I haven't set foot in it yet, but you live here. What do you think of it?" Other questions were serious. "Do you regret the sacrifice of your life to the natives of Africa?" Albert replied, "There was no sacrifice. I am one of the greatly privileged."

Wherever they went in the United States, Albert and Hélène found their fame had gone before them. Two years earlier, Americans Charles Joy and Melvin Arnold had visited Lambaréné. Charles had taken over a thousand photographs, while Melvin had taken extensive notes. When they returned home, they wrote a book titled *The Africa of Albert Schweitzer.* The book was hugely popular, and as a result, Albert Schweitzer had become a household name in the United States. Albert became even more recognizable when *Time* magazine featured a painting of him on the cover of the July 11, 1949, issue. Beneath his portrait were the words "He who loses his life shall find it." Inside the magazine was a long article titled "Reverence for Life," which told the story of Albert and his work at Lambaréné.

By the time the article was published, Albert and Hélène had taken the long train ride from New York to Aspen, where Albert gave his Goethe speech twice, once in French and again in German. The event was a great success, and more articles about Albert followed in America's most popular publications. *Reader's Digest* published two articles. The first was "God's Eager Fool" by the Reverend John O'Brien, who wrote, "Nearly 2,000 years ago St. Paul spoke of those who are 'fools for Christ's sake.' Since then many men and women have marched down history, yielding up the comforts of life to serve their fellow men. With that bright company today goes that eager fool for God—Albert Schweitzer."

The second article that *Reader's Digest* published was written by Albert and appeared in the same issue. Albert titled the article "Your Second Job" and used it to call people to look for opportunities in their lives to have a second job. In the article he explained,

> What the world lacks most today is men who occupy themselves with the needs of other men. In this unselfish labor a blessing falls on both the helper and the helped. Without such spiritual adventures the man or woman of today walks in darkness. . . . What is the remedy? No matter how busy one is, any human being can assert his personality by seizing every opportunity for spiritual activity. How? By his second job; by means of personal action, on however small a scale, for the good of his fellow men.

By October 1949 Albert was Le Grand Docteur back in Lambaréné, once more overseeing the hospital and staff. He had taken a large supply of sulfone drugs back with him and dreamed of eliminating leprosy around Lambaréné and the riverside villages of the Ogowe. News traveled fast. Within months sixty people suffering from leprosy were lining up for weekly shots of the sulfone drugs. Albert also broke ground on the leprosy village at a site a seven-minute walk from the hospital. Temporary bamboo huts were erected while Albert gathered the materials to build permanent structures on the site. Hearing of the new village, more people with leprosy arrived, some from up to 250 miles away. By the end of 1953, over three hundred people were receiving treatment for leprosy.

Albert was desperately trying to find a way to get better housing at the leprosy village when he was notified he'd been awarded the prestigious Nobel Peace Prize for service to humanity. During the selection process for the prize in 1952, the Nobel Committee had decided that none of that year's nominees met the criteria Alfred Nobel had laid out, and so they did not award the peace prize. A year later in 1953, after the selection process, the committee ended up with two suitable candidates for the prize. The committee decided to retrospectively award the 1952 Nobel Peace Prize to Albert. Not only was it a distinguished honor, but also it came with a cash prize of $30,000, all of which Albert immediately donated to building a better leprosy village and a radiography building.

Albert traveled to Oslo, Norway, where Hélène joined him. On November 4, 1954, he gave his acceptance speech for the peace prize in the presence of King Gustav of Norway. Albert's address was titled "The Problem of Peace," and he ended it by saying, "May those who have in their hands the fate of nations take anxious care to avoid whatever may worsen our situation and make it more dangerous. And may they take to heart the words of the Apostle Paul: 'If it be possible, as much as lieth in you, live peaceably with all men.' His words are valid not only for individuals but for whole nations as well."

The following evening Albert and Hélène stood side by side on the balcony of the town hall as hundreds of university students honored them with a candlelight procession. It was a magical moment that Albert would never forget. *LIFE* magazine featured a story on Albert Schweitzer titled "A Man of Mercy," accompanied with photographs by renowned photographer W. Eugene Smith.

A month later, Albert headed back to Lambaréné with what he considered the true prize—five tons of equipment for the leprosy village. Hélène didn't return with him. In December 1954 she had heart problems and decided to stay a little longer in Europe with Rhena and the grandchildren. She arrived back in Lambaréné in January 1955 in time to celebrate Albert's eightieth birthday on January 14. Eleven days later, Hélène celebrated her seventy-sixth birthday.

The following August Albert and Hélène returned to France to spend the fall in Alsace. Albert also traveled to London, England, where on October 17, 1955, he was awarded the Order of Merit by Queen Elizabeth II of Great Britain. Albert was the ninety-ninth person to be awarded the honor since its inception in 1902. Albert also dined with British Prime Minister Anthony Eden at his official resident at 10 Downing Street and accepted an honorary doctorate from Cambridge University. By now he'd lost count of the number of honorary degrees that had been conferred on him.

As usual, Albert didn't stay away from Lambaréné for long. He returned before Christmas, and Hélène joined him there in January 1956. By now Albert was aware that his wife was very frail and ill. The woman who'd once worked so energetically by his side lay listlessly on a sofa on the veranda, watching the comings and goings of the hospital she had helped found. What little energy she had, she spent helping Albert prepare a speech titled "Peace or Atomic War." Albert had become increasingly concerned about atomic war. He'd seen the horrific pictures and movie clips of the utter devastation and death that had occurred when the atomic bombs were dropped on the Japanese cities of Hiroshima and Nagasaki to end World War II.

Throughout his life Albert had witnessed firsthand how fickle world leaders were when it came to war. He hated to think what might become of humanity if people had the potential to push a button and destroy entire nations as they had destroyed cities in Japan. As a result, he felt he must speak out on the issue. Albert's speech was broadcast worldwide by radio on April 23, 1956. He ended it with a plea. "The end of further experiments with atom bombs would be like the early sunrays of hope which suffering humanity is longing for."

The following month Hélène decided she needed to return to the cooler climate of Europe if she was to have any hope of living longer. As Albert said goodbye to her on May 22, he realized it could well be his final goodbye to his wife. Hélène and the nurse accompanying her on the journey traveled by road to Brazzaville, where they boarded an airplane and flew to Paris. This made the trip astonishingly fast.

Hélène Schweitzer Bresslau died on June 1, 1957, of heart disease. Albert received a telegram in Lambaréné from Rhena giving him the sad news.

Albert arrived in Switzerland a month later. He collected his wife's ashes and returned to Africa. On the hospital grounds in Lambaréné, Albert buried Hélène's ashes beneath a cross he had carved. While he was at it, he carved a matching cross for himself.

At eighty-two Albert was still in robust health, though he no longer supervised patients every day and filled in on hospital rounds only when it was necessary. The hospital's sprawling gardens and orchards were now Albert's pride and joy, and he found great satisfaction tending them.

Although he'd given up traveling, Albert still retained an active interest in world affairs. He was particularly supportive of the movement to ban the more powerful atomic weapons now being tested, and he regularly corresponded with Albert Einstein on the matter.

Before his ninetieth birthday on January 14, 1965, Albert invited his daughter to join him. He and Rhena shared the same birthday but were seldom together to celebrate it. Rhena arrived at Lambaréné in time for the joint celebration. Albert was proud of his daughter. Rhena had returned to school to become a laboratory technician, and she had agreed to stay at Lambaréné and supervise the laboratory.

Albert remained in good health until late August, when he began tiring easily. With Rhena at his side, Le Grand Docteur died peacefully in his bed at 10:30 p.m. on Saturday, September 4, 1965. His final words were "There is still much work to be done."

Dr. Albert Louis Philipp Schweitzer's body was wrapped in cloth and lowered into a grave beside Hélène. Many hands spread palm leaves over him before his body was covered with dirt. It was the same dirt from which he had extracted massive roots; dirt into which he had hammered piles and planted trees, and which he had cleaned off the bodies of thousands of patients over the years. His body lay at rest exactly where he wanted it, in a simple grave in the place where he had served faithfully for fifty years.

"The only thing of importance, when we depart, will be the traces of love we have left behind."

—Albert Schweitzer

Bibliography

Anderson, Erica. *The Schweitzer Album*. New York: Harper & Row, 1965.

Bentley, James. *Albert Schweitzer: The Enigma*. New York: HarperCollins, 1992.

Berman, Edgar, Dr. *In Africa with Schweitzer*. Far Hills, NJ: New Horizon Press, 1986.

Franck, Frederick. *Days with Albert Schweitzer: A Lambaréné Landscape*. New York: Holt, 1959.

Gire, Ken. *Answering the Call: The Doctor Who Made Africa His Life*. Nashville: Thomas Nelson, 2013.

Joy, Charles R., and Melvin Arnold. *The Africa of Albert Schweitzer*. Boston: Beacon Press, 1948.

Marxsen, Patti M. *Helene Schweitzer: A Life of Her Own*. Syracuse, NY: Syracuse University Press, 2015.

Manton, Jo. *The Story of Albert Schweitzer*. New York: Abelard-Schuman, 1955.

Oermann, Nils Ole. *Albert Schweitzer: A Biography*. Oxford: Oxford University Press, 2017.

Payne, Robert. *The Three Worlds of Albert Schweitzer*. New York: Thomas Nelson, 1957.

Schweitzer, Albert. *Letters: 1905–1965*. New York: Macmillan, 1992.

———. *On the Edge of the Primeval Forest*. New York: Macmillan, 1948.

———. *Out of My Life and Thought: An Autobiography.* New York: Holt, 1949.

Seaver, George. *Albert Schweitzer: The Man and His Mind*. New York: Harper & Brothers, 1947.

About the Authors

Janet and Geoff Benge are a husband and wife writing team with more than thirty years of writing experience. Janet is a former elementary school teacher. Geoff holds a degree in history. Originally from New Zealand, the Benges spent ten years serving with Youth With A Mission. They have two daughters, Laura and Shannon, and an adopted son, Lito. They make their home in the Orlando, Florida, area.

Christian Heroes: Then & Now are available in paperback, e-book, and audiobook formats, with more coming soon!

www.YWAMpublishing.com

Also from Janet and Geoff Benge...

More adventure-filled biographies for ages 10 to 100!

Christian Heroes: Then and Now

Gladys Aylward: The Adventure of a Lifetime • 978-1-57658-019-6
Nate Saint: On a Wing and a Prayer • 978-1-57658-017-2
Hudson Taylor: Deep in the Heart of China • 978-1-57658-016-5
Amy Carmichael: Rescuer of Precious Gems • 978-1-57658-018-9
Eric Liddell: Something Greater Than Gold • 978-1-57658-137-7
Corrie ten Boom: Keeper of the Angels' Den • 978-1-57658-136-0
William Carey: Obliged to Go • 978-1-57658-147-6
George Müller: Guardian of Bristol's Orphans • 978-1-57658-145-2
Jim Elliot: One Great Purpose • 978-1-57658-146-9
Mary Slessor: Forward into Calabar • 978-1-57658-148-3
David Livingstone: Africa's Trailblazer • 978-1-57658-153-7
Betty Greene: Wings to Serve • 978-1-57658-152-0
Adoniram Judson: Bound for Burma • 978-1-57658-161-2
Cameron Townsend: Good News in Every Language • 978-1-57658-164-3
Jonathan Goforth: An Open Door in China • 978-1-57658-174-2
Lottie Moon: Giving Her All for China • 978-1-57658-188-9
John Williams: Messenger of Peace • 978-1-57658-256-5
William Booth: Soup, Soap, and Salvation • 978-1-57658-258-9
Rowland Bingham: Into Africa's Interior • 978-1-57658-282-4
Ida Scudder: Healing Bodies, Touching Hearts • 978-1-57658-285-5
Wilfred Grenfell: Fisher of Men • 978-1-57658-292-3
Lillian Trasher: The Greatest Wonder in Egypt • 978-1-57658-305-0
Loren Cunningham: Into All the World • 978-1-57658-199-5
Florence Young: Mission Accomplished • 978-1-57658-313-5
Sundar Singh: Footprints Over the Mountains • 978-1-57658-318-0
C.T. Studd: No Retreat • 978-1-57658-288-6
Rachel Saint: A Star in the Jungle • 978-1-57658-337-1
Brother Andrew: God's Secret Agent • 978-1-57658-355-5
Clarence Jones: Mr. Radio • 978-1-57658-343-2
Count Zinzendorf: Firstfruit • 978-1-57658-262-6
John Wesley: The World His Parish • 978-1-57658-382-1
C. S. Lewis: Master Storyteller • 978-1-57658-385-2
David Bussau: Facing the World Head-on • 978-1-57658-415-6
Jacob DeShazer: Forgive Your Enemies • 978-1-57658-475-0
Isobel Kuhn: On the Roof of the World • 978-1-57658-497-2
Elisabeth Elliot: Joyful Surrender • 978-1-57658-513-9
D. L. Moody: Bringing Souls to Christ • 978-1-57658-552-8
Paul Brand: Helping Hands • 978-1-57658-536-8
Dietrich Bonhoeffer: In the Midst of Wickedness • 978-1-57658-713-3
Francis Asbury: Circuit Rider • 978-1-57658-737-9

Samuel Zwemer: The Burden of Arabia • 978-1-57658-738-6
Klaus-Dieter John: Hope in the Land of the Incas • 978-1-57658-826-2
Mildred Cable: Through the Jade Gate • 978-1-57658-886-4
John Flynn: Into the Never Never • 978-1-57658-898-7
Richard Wurmbrand: Love Your Enemies • 978-1-57658-987-8
Charles Mulli: We Are Family • 978-1-57658-894-9
John Newton: Change of Heart • 978-1-57658-909-0
Helen Roseveare: Mama Luka • 978-1-57658-910-6
Norman Grubb: Mission Builder • 978-1-57658-915-1
Albert Schweitzer • 978-1-57658-961-8

Heroes of History

George Washington Carver: From Slave to Scientist • 978-1-883002-78-7
Abraham Lincoln: A New Birth of Freedom • 978-1-883002-79-4
Meriwether Lewis: Off the Edge of the Map • 978-1-883002-80-0
George Washington: True Patriot • 978-1-883002-81-7
William Penn: Liberty and Justice for All • 978-1-883002-82-4
Harriet Tubman: Freedombound • 978-1-883002-90-9
John Adams: Independence Forever • 978-1-883002-50-3
Clara Barton: Courage under Fire • 978-1-883002-51-0
Daniel Boone: Frontiersman • 978-1-932096-09-5
Theodore Roosevelt: An American Original • 978-1-932096-10-1
Douglas MacArthur: What Greater Honor • 978-1-932096-15-6
Benjamin Franklin: Live Wire • 978-1-932096-14-9
Christopher Columbus: Across the Ocean Sea • 978-1-932096-23-1
Laura Ingalls Wilder: A Storybook Life • 978-1-932096-32-3
Orville Wright: The Flyer • 978-1-932096-34-7
Captain John Smith: A Foothold in the New World • 978-1-932096-36-1
Thomas Edison: Inspiration and Hard Work • 978-1-932096-37-8
Alan Shepard: Higher and Faster • 978-1-932096-41-5
Ronald Reagan: Destiny at His Side • 978-1-932096-65-1
Davy Crockett: Ever Westward • 978-1-932096-67-5
Milton Hershey: More Than Chocolate • 978-1-932096-82-8
Billy Graham: America's Pastor • 978-1-62486-024-9
Ben Carson: A Chance at Life • 978-1-62486-034-8
Louis Zamperini: Redemption • 978-1-62486-049-2
Elizabeth Fry: Angel of Newgate • 978-1-62486-064-5
William Wilberforce: Take Up the Fight • 978-1-62486-057-7
William Bradford: Plymouth's Rock • 978-1-62486-092-8
Ernest Shackleton: Going South • 978-1-62486-093-5
Benjamin Rush: The Common Good • 978-1-62486-123-9